T0232286

Lecture Notes in Computer Science

Lecture Notes in Computer Science

Edited by G. Goos and J. Hartmanis

234

Concepts in User Interfaces:
A Reference Model for
Command and Response
Languages

By Members of IFIP Working Group 2.7:
David Beech, Christian Gram, Hans-Jürgen Kugler,
Ian Newman, Helmut Stiegler, and Claus Unger

Edited by David Beech

Springer-Verlag
Berlin Heidelberg New York London Paris Tokyo

Editorial Board

D. Barstow W. Brauer P. Brinch Hansen D. Gries D. Luckham
C. Moler A. Pnueli G. Seegmüller J. Stoer N. Wirth

Editor

David Beech
Chairman of IFIP WG 2.7
Hewlett-Packard Laboratories
1501 Page Mill Road, Palo Alto, CA 94304, USA

This monograph presents results developed by
Working Group 2.7 (Operating System Interfaces)
of the International Federation for Information
Processing (IFIP); the authors are:

D. Beech	Hewlett-Packard Laboratories, Palo Alto, USA
C. Gram	Technical University of Denmark, Lyngby, Denmark
H. J. Kugler	Trinity College, Dublin, Ireland
I. Newman	Loughborough University of Technology, United Kingdom
H. G. Stiegler	Siemens AG, Munich, Federal Republic of Germany
C. Unger	FernUniversität, Hagen, Federal Republic of Germany

CR Subject Classifications (1985): H.1.2

ISBN 3-540-16791-9 Springer-Verlag Berlin Heidelberg New York
ISBN 0-387-16791-9 Springer-Verlag New York Berlin Heidelberg

This work is subject to copyright. All rights are reserved, whether the whole or part of the material
is concerned, specifically those of translation, reprinting, re-use of illustrations, broadcasting,
reproduction by photocopying machine or similar means, and storage in data banks. Under
§ 54 of the German Copyright Law where copies are made for other than private use, a fee is
payable to "Verwertungsgesellschaft Wort", Munich.

© Springer-Verlag Berlin Heidelberg 1986
Printed in Germany

Printing and binding: Beltz Offsetdruck, Hemsbach/Bergstr.

Preface

Users of computer systems are greeted nowadays by a bewildering variety of interfaces. Different systems, often accessed in rapid succession via networks, require the user to remember different ways of doing the same thing; and alternative media, such as keyboard, mouse, touch screen, and telephone, add another dimension of variety and complexity. There is a need for a clear conceptual framework which could lead to better tutorial exposition of existing interfaces, to improved new interfaces, and even to the design of a high-quality standard which could provide a uniform interface to different systems.

As a first step in this direction, the present document attempts to identify and describe some appropriate concepts, and put them together in the form of an abstract model which should serve as a useful reference for anyone interested in obtaining a better understanding or bringing about improvements in this area. It is hoped that it may immediately help communication of ideas by offering a common model, terminology and method of description. Thereafter, it can be applied not only to the design of new systems, but also in specifying improved or standard interfaces to existing systems. Because of the urgency of addressing the latter problems, it has seemed preferable to offer the model as a contribution in its present state rather than to delay publication in order to develop it further.

The term "reference model" was first popularised by the Open Systems Interconnection reference model [1], which aimed to establish a framework for the development of standards. The present model is related to the OSI model, but its nature and intent are somewhat different, emphasising the organisation of concepts rather than the structure of the standards process. Another interesting relationship is to the object-oriented user interface model being developed for the Portable Common Tool Environment [2].

Salient features of the present reference model are that

- it is user-oriented, with an emphasis on modelling the semantics of systems as perceivable at their user interfaces, rather than modelling the underlying implementation structures;

- it employs the object concept, defining types of object and their semantics by the method of data abstraction;

- it encourages the separation of concerns between the semantics of the canonical (abstract) form of a "command" and "response" provided by a system, and the mechanisms for customising the external (concrete) forms they may take for various media and users. This is important, both in designing new applications and systems, and also in improving existing systems, and developing standards:

  — for new systems, there is a trend towards the provision of separable user interface management systems, handling the user interface to application programs as well as to system functions, thus easing application development and encouraging quality and consistency across the complete user interface;

— a key factor in improving existing interfaces is to be able to escape from the influence of the cardpunch and typewriter modes of input, and make the interfaces adaptable to new media, to usage in different parts of the world, and to the individual user, without having the freedom to change the underlying system semantics;

— comparison of semantics would be a crucial part of the design of a standard which aimed to be implementable on major existing systems—the feasibility of such a standard would depend on the ability to specify an implementable set of canonical forms, following which it would become worthwhile to define corresponding external forms.

This reference model has been constructed by Working Group 2.7 of the International Federation for Information Processing, the principal authors being:

D. Beech   Hewlett-Packard Laboratories, Palo Alto, USA
C. Gram   Technical University of Denmark, Lyngby, Denmark
H.J. Kugler   Trinity College, Dublin, Ireland
I. Newman   Loughborough University of Technology, United Kingdom
H.G. Stiegler Siemens AG, Munich, West Germany
C. Unger   FernUniversität, Hagen, West Germany

Other members and observers who have contributed to this work are J. Coutaz (France), I. Dahlstrand (Sweden), R. Dakin (Australia), B. Dautrevaux (France), T.A. Dolotta (USA), L.C. Frampton (USA), F. Gallo (Italy), S. Hegner (USA), K. Hopper (New Zealand), L. Keedy (Australia), A. Langsford (UK), J. Larson (USA), M. Mac an Airchinnigh (Ireland), J.B. McKeehan (USA), J. Madsen (Denmark), K.V. Nori (India), R.A. Pocock (USA), and H.J. Weegenaar (Netherlands). The final stages have also benefitted from the helpful comments of the editor of the Lecture Notes in Computer Science, Dr. G. Goos.

The Working Group would especially like to record its gratitude to Rosalie Pocock, whose dedication as secretary of the group since 1977 has enabled this work to be carried through.

IFIP Working Group 2.7 was founded in 1975 under the chairmanship of F.R. Hertweck (W. Germany). The charter of the group is to address questions related to Operating Systems Interfaces, and the main interest has been in general-purpose user interfaces taking the form of Command and Response Languages. Three IFIP Working Conferences have been held on this topic, with proceedings published as follows:

Unger, C. (ed): Command Languages.   North Holland (1975).

Beech, D. (ed): Command Language Directions.   North Holland (1980).

Hopper, K. and Newman, I. (eds): Foundations for Human-Computer Communication.
                                   North Holland (1986).

Further information about the group and its activities is obtainable from: Dr. R. A. Pocock, AT&T International (Japan) Ltd., Nippon Press Center Building, 2-1, Uchisaiwai-cho, 2-chome, Chiyoda-ku, Tokyo 100, Japan.

                                    D. Beech
Palo Alto, California   *Chairman, IFIP WG 2.7,*
June, 1986   *Editor*

Contents

A REFERENCE MODEL FOR
COMMAND AND RESPONSE LANGUAGES

1. Introduction

1.1 Nature and Intent of the Reference Model

This Reference Model provides a conceptual framework for the understanding and development of the kind of user interface to a computer system which has generally been known as a *command language*, or more fully as an *Operating System Command and Response Language* (OSCRL). Such an interface essentially exercises the general-purpose facilities of a system rather than its specialised applications, with the user issuing a command and the system responding with an indication of success or failure. In the past, the command and response have often resembled sentences in a language, but this reference model is intended to cover the generalisation to multi-media inputs and outputs, which might for example involve icon selection on a display or use of a touchtone phone to construct a command, and a flashing sign or audible message as the response.

Reference models are becoming popular as a means of conceptual organisation, but they differ somewhat in their nature and intent, so that it is important to clarify who might use the model as a reference, and what is being modelled. In this case, the model is offered as an aid to anyone studying or comparing existing command and response languages, carrying out research or designing new languages, or perhaps all of these in attempting to formulate a standard which will be forward-looking, and yet be implementable on existing systems. The nature of the model may be illustrated by considering its use by the designer of a specific language based on the reference model, who would ultimately define a representation (e.g. a syntax) for commands and responses, and would express the semantics of commands in terms of the concepts of the model. (This process will be illustrated later, in the chapter on "Application of the Reference Model".) Thus the *reference model* does not itself define a language, but provides a conceptual quarry from which the designer may select and fashion parts and combine them with other components in producing a *definitive model* of a specific language, which would be analogous to an operational semantic definition of a programming language. From the definitive model, simplified *user-oriented models* could be derived to give appropriate help to various classes of users, whereas the corresponding *implementation models* for User Interface Management Systems (UIMS) would typically need to be more complex, with lower-level detail and special mechanisms for optimising performance. It should be emphasised that this document does not describe an implementation model, although of course some of the concepts may be implemented using similar structures to those of the reference model.

Thus the general intent of this reference model is that it should help to improve the quality, the flexibility, the design methodology, and, as far as possible and desirable, the uniformity of command and response languages, by providing descriptions of a set of fundamental concepts which are independent of the details of any particular language or implementation.

1.2 Scope of the Reference Model

The scope of the reference model will be indicated in the following subsections by describing, from the designer's point of view, the general class of systems and languages to which the model is applicable.

1.2.1 Users and Systems

A human user of a computer system is considered to be outside the system, and possibly to be one of many concurrent users of the system. Inanimate users are also provided for, being either other systems external to the given system, or programs within the system which wish to use the services available to external users. The system with which the user deals is an entity providing a set of services, and need only be understood at a level of detail relevant to those services. From other points of view, it may be a part of a larger system, or may be composed of a network of smaller systems.

A system has one or more *access points* at which information can pass between the external user and the system in either direction. An access point could, for example, be a typewriter terminal connected to a time-sharing system, or the keyboard together with the display of a personal computer, or a telephone, or a connection to another system.

The most general description of a system in these terms is that it is capable of:

- accepting inputs from external users at one or more access points, and generating outputs at one or more access points;

- remembering information which could later be retrieved, or could in some other way influence future output of the system (the totality of such information at any time will be called the *state* of the system);

- performing computations which transform the information within the system.

1.2.2 Commands and Responses

In order for an external user to instruct a general-purpose system what it is to do, a command and response language is provided. *Commands* are a form of input which may cause the generation of one or more outputs, or a change in the state of the system, or both. The outputs may be directly derived from the previous state of the system, or may involve computation by the system. One of the outputs, normally produced at the same access point as received the command, may be designated as a *response*.

The effects of certain commands, including the resulting responses, are specified as part of the semantics of the command and response language. Other commands may use arbitrary services of a system, or user-written programs, whose semantics are not understood by the command and response language. Some commands may be composite, causing the execution of a succession of commands, possibly with program activity interspersed between them.

1.2.3 Customisation and Help

The command and response language may be customised to suit particular users. We shall say that each command is executed, and each response is generated, within a specific *context*, so that, for example, commands and responses may be adapted to the user's own natural language, and the significance of names used in commands may depend on the current context. Other forms of customisation may depend on the nature of the access point, with perhaps two-dimensional menu selection of commands being provided on a display terminal, or touchtone commands and audible responses on a telephone.

The user should be able to seek help in constructing commands and understanding responses, and even in solving problems during execution of a command when necessary. The help facilities may be customised to the user and access point by means of information in the current context.

The facilities for customisation and help thus influence a language in two ways: they affect all commands and responses in the language, and also require the provision of commands specially to control the customisation and help facilities themselves.

1.2.4 Invocation of System Services

Once the significance of a command has been determined within the user's context, the command has to be obeyed. If its effect is not purely local to the workings of the command and response language, some service of the underlying system must be invoked. During the performance of this system service, the semantics may be defined by the particular service, and may involve a dialogue with the user via the same access point as that from which the command was issued. This dialogue may take advantage of the customisation and help facilities discussed earlier, in order to provide consistency in the user interface.

1.2.5 Sharing of System Services

The services and information provided by a system to multiple users will in general need to be shared in a carefully controlled way. The two main aspects of this are the protection of information and services from undesired access and usage by others, and the prevention of undesired interference from concurrent activity by different users who are allowed access.

By analogy with the discussion of customisation and help above, this has two implications for command and response languages: every command is subject to the protection rules and concurrency control of the system, and the language may also contain commands whose role is specifically to affect the way these controls are applied.

A system available to multiple users will usually wish to authenticate a user before allowing extensive access to its services. Successful authentication allows an appropriate context to be provided for the user.

1.2.6 Concurrent Usage

The activities of a system may proceed concurrently in various ways (or may appear to users to do so). Concurrent execution of commands may take place in different local systems in a network, or in a single local system with several access points, or in several tasks of a user at a single access point.

Where such commands attempt to perform concurrent operations on the same object, some operations may be designed to permit this while others need serialisation.

If conflicts such as deadlock situations arise, the system should attempt automatic recovery where possible, but the user may be aware of this or may be required to assist in the recovery process in some systems.

1.3 The Object Concept

The unifying concept of the model is that of the *object*, in the sense used in data abstraction [3-6]. This section will introduce the concept informally and show how it relates to command and response languages.

At the highest level of abstraction, a complete system can be thought of as a single object with which users (human or otherwise) may communicate by issuing commands and receiving responses. We should then like to be able to describe the effect of the commands on the behaviour of the system, i.e., on the responses and other outputs that could be generated in the future, without knowing all the details of the interior of the system. Since an output will in general depend not only on the command most recently issued, but also on the past history of the system, it is convenient to think of the state of the system object as representing the necessary memory of its history. The effect of a command is in general to alter the state and to return a response, possibly with other inputs and outputs intervening.

The system is thus a "black box" in the sense that its actual internal mechanisms are supposed to be unknown, and its behaviour can be observed only in terms of its outputs, such as the responses it gives to commands. There are various ways in which the specifications for such a system can be given, and the method that we shall employ is to populate the interior of the system with some hypothetical objects (Figure 1) whose interactions will produce the desired effects. There is no obligation for an actual implementation of a system specified like this to use the same methods, provided that, for any given initial state and sequence of inputs, it will produce exactly the specified outputs interleaved in the specified sequence between the inputs.

Objects can perform *operations* on other objects, and receive *results* from them, as illustrated by the arrows on the left of the boxes. The objects operated upon may also suffer state changes. The operations and results are all part of a hypothetical internal mechanism.

Commands and responses are particular kinds of inputs and outputs crossing the system boundary, and internal objects may also cause other kinds of inputs and outputs across the boundary in the time between the issuing of a command and the receipt of its response.

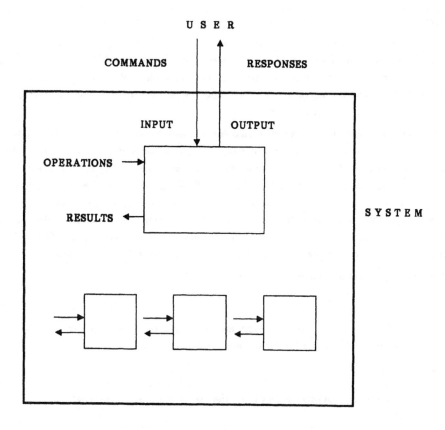

Figure 1. A system populated by internal objects.

Objects are classified into *types*, where each type defines what operations are permissible on the objects which are *instances* of that type. The description of an operation involves both a definition of the interface through which it may be invoked and may return its result (much like a procedure declaration), and the semantic specification of the effects of applying the operation (the abstract equivalent of a procedure body).

The semantics of an operation may often be described in terms of operations on objects of other types, or of the same type, but ultimately the definition must rest on some primitive operations which are understood by other means, such as well-known mathematical functions or operations described in natural language.

1.4 Notation

Each type of object is defined as an abstract data type specifying its structure and the basic operations permissible on objects of that type. Every type and operation is described in English, and in addition a formal notation is used, which is based on a blend of the Vienna Development Method (VDM) [7] and the Affirm specification language [8]. For a detailed description of the formal notation, please see Appendices A and B.

The VDM metalanguage is used to specify each operation, and the notation of Affirm is introduced to group the operations into object types (corresponding to semantic domains in VDM). Where the formal specification is felt to be too complex to give a good understanding of the concept under consideration, only a description in English is given. All the operations are specified as functions in the applicative style, but it is understood that, in an actual implementation, some operations (such as InsertEntry and RemoveEntry on the Directory type) may work in an imperative way by actually changing the state of the objects in question. Note also that objects like the ContextTree and the BondedStore may be considered as elements of the global state of the system.

An object type specification contains the sections:

TYPE

defines the name of the new type, and possibly also a type expression defining a data structure for the new type.

NEEDS TYPES

contains a list of other object types that are used in the present specification.

DECLARE

is a declaration of identifiers denoting instances of objects used as arguments in the INTERFACES section.

INTERFACES

contains names and type specifications of functions defining the basic operations permissible on the new type.

END

A section may be omitted if it is not necessary for a given object type—for example, the INTERFACES section will not be specified when only the default operations are available. Default operations are provided to create and delete an instance, get and set the component objects of a type defined by means of a VDM structured object, or to carry out the VDM operations on sets or lists for types which are defined by those means.

A simple error mechanism is provided, whereby an operation which should return a result of type T may return a special error instance of the type. A function of the form ErrorT to create such an instance, and a Boolean function of the form IsErrorT to test for it, is available for each T. If an object x satisfying IsErrorT(x) is passed as an input parameter to another operation expecting a parameter of type T, and producing a result of type U, the result will be ErrorU. Note that in all uses within this reference model, functions like ErrorU take no arguments, and thus their invocations look syntactically like references to a special object. Designs of actual command and response languages will need a more refined mechanism to differentiate between errors and generate appropriate responses, for example by parameterising the ErrorU functions and having WhichErrorU functions to discriminate between the resulting error objects.

2. Overview of the Reference Model

This chapter provides a general overview of the reference model, and the next chapter illustrates how a designer might apply the model. Chapters 4-13 then describe the model in full, and two appendices define the metalanguage of the document.

The first section of the present chapter discusses the modelling of systems and their boundaries. The following seven sections then introduce the main features of the reference model. In the final section, some constraints are placed on the initial state of the system assumed by the detailed definitions of object types and operations in the succeeding chapters.

2.1 Systems, Access Points and Networks

At the highest level of abstraction, the reference model shows the possibility of multiple users communicating with a single system. Such a system might be connected into a network of systems. It might even itself consist of a network of systems at a lower level of abstraction which could be ignored in modelling commands which made that network appear to the user as a single system.

A system communicates with the world outside itself through access points. Each access point is associated with some interior object, and the model will concern itself especially with access points that support a Command and Response Language (*CRL*) based on the reference model. Each such access point is associated with an instance of a Transmitter object, as illustrated in Figure 2. The user might be human, or might be another system communicating with this one via a command and response language—possibly in a specially customised form. (A natural extension of the model could be made to handle other forms of communication between systems, as structured in the Open Systems Interconnection Architecture standard [1]. For example, an Interconnection type of object could be defined, with an instance in each system, and operations corresponding to the services of the Application Layer which could be invoked by operations on other objects in the system when interconnection was necessary.)

In practical terms, the user is assumed to have done his or her part in whatever is physically necessary for the access point to become active, such as switching on a terminal, dialling a phone number, and pressing certain keys on a keyboard, before the reference model begins to define the structure of the interactions.

2.2 CRL Processors, Transmitters and Contexts

The initial state of the system, with respect to such a user who is just about to begin a *session*, is dominated by a trio of objects: a CRLProcessor, which is associated with the Transmitter at the user's access point, and with a Context. (A dotted arc from one object to another in Figure 2 shows that the first object contains information equivalent to a reference to the second. Solid lines indicate data flow.) The system is also populated by many other objects of various types, some of which will be described in detail in the reference model, while others are quite arbitrary as far as the command and response language is concerned.

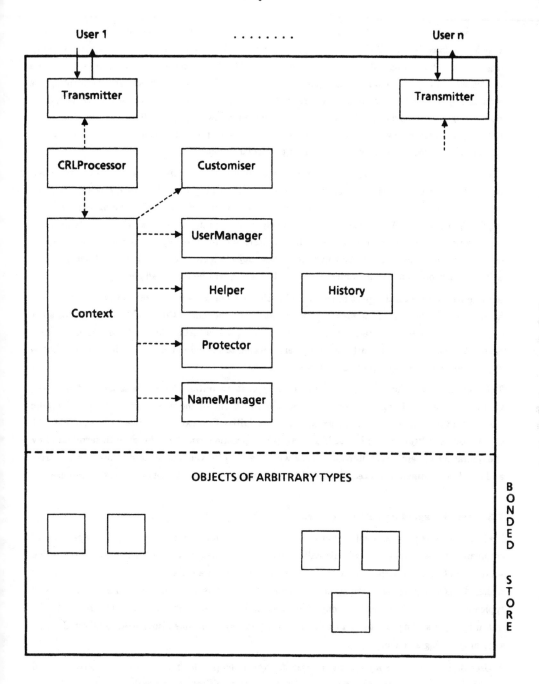

Figure 2. The main components of the reference model.

The exact means by which the above trio of objects may be established is via an Activate operation which is defined for the CRLProcessor type, to which a Transmitter and a Context are passed as arguments. Thus an operating system might determine which access points were to be initialised in this way to expect commands as inputs, by creating CRLProcessor objects and performing the Activate operation to bind them to appropriate access points and initial Contexts. Other access points might be associated with objects which served as switches and offered the user a choice between different subsystems (and their command and response languages). Still other access points might provide dedicated interfaces to particular applications.

During a session, a CRLProcessor is always associated with a *Context* object defining the environment in which the user is currently operating. (In describing operations within the model, this *current Context* of the session is assumed to be globally known rather than being passed as an explicit parameter.) A Context object effectively contains references to several objects of other types which define the services available to the user, and the possibly customised form in which commands and responses may be conveyed. These objects include a Customiser, a UserManager, a Helper, a Protector, and a NameManager, all of which will be described shortly.

An important structural aspect of the model is that a Context is in general composite. A system has a *ContextTree* with an *ElementaryContext* at each node, and a Context then consists of a list of ElementaryContexts corresponding to some path upwards in the ContextTree. Thus the first ElementaryContext in the path might be very specific to an individual user, whereas the next is applicable to a whole group or project, and so forth.

The Activate operation mentioned above ensures that an *initial Context* is associated with the CRLProcessor, providing an environment within which one or more selected commands may be executed by any user at that access point. This initial Context determines, for example, the Customiser and Protector to be used. The Activate operation essentially loops until terminated by the operating system. Each iteration seeks with the aid of a Customiser and Protector to derive and check a Command, to execute it, and to transmit a customised Response back to the user.

2.3 UserManagers and KnownUsers

Many systems require authentication of a user before permitting any considerable repertoire of commands to be employed, and this will be modelled by means of a *UserManager* object which serves to determine whether the user should be provided with a more generous Context. (Systems which do not require authentication may omit this checking.) Thus the current Context will typically be switched to another Context by a successful "login" command, and will revert to the initial Context at "logout" to await another user. Some systems may also provide explicit Context switching during a session.

A UserManager contains a mapping of *UserIdentifications* (i.e. login names) to *KnownUsers*, and the FindKnownUser operation will find the KnownUser object corresponding to a given User-Identification. A system may employ one UserManager for all Contexts, or it may employ different UserManagers to limit the availability of certain access points to selected groups of users. Once the desired KnownUser has been found in the UserManager, more information becomes available and can be validated, such as a password which might be required.

To avoid misunderstanding, the terminology "known user" should be clarified. The system knows what it has been told, for example by a system administrator, about the potential users of the system and their characteristics. It is this information which is contained in KnownUser objects. An actual user has to convince the system that he, she or it fits the description of a KnownUser, but the system has no direct means of distinguishing between actual users, and the correspondence between actual and known users may be many-to-many. Each Context contains a reference both to the associated UserManager and to the particular KnownUser who is active within that Context. In the case of an initial Context prior to "login", the KnownUser will be system-provided with an identifier which may be kept private within the system, and this is the sense in which we shall say that there is an "anonymous user" at that point.

The KnownUser object is the focal point for information about a specific user. Besides the means of authentication, there is, for example, a *UserProfile* which enables a suitable Context to be established on completion of "login".

2.4 Customisers, Commands and Responses

The DeriveCommand operation on a *Customiser* object translates user commands—submitted in a form particular to the user and the nature of the access point—into a canonical form whose semantics can then be specified in terms of operations on other objects. In fact, the initial input received by the Customiser from the Transmitter may not be a complete or valid command, or it may be several commands. At the stage when it is received from the Transmitter, the input is therefore described merely as a *Message*. DeriveCommand may then perform operations on the Transmitter to engage in dialogue with the user if necessary, or it may stack unused inputs for later use. Using information available via the current Context, a canonical form of a single command will be produced and returned to the CRLProcessor in a *Command* object.

The CustomiseResponse operation works in the reverse direction, receiving a canonical form of *Response*, and using information available via the current Context to adapt it, for example to the natural language of the user and to a spoken form to be heard on a telephone, before sending the appropriate Message to the Transmitter.

2.5 Helpers and Histories

Operations on a *Helper* may give information on such topics as what commands are available, how to do and undo commands, how to escape from seemingly desperate situations, how to perform tasks of a more general kind than given by a single command, or the status of the current context or session. The importance attached to the provision of help is indicated in the reference model by the extensive functional requirements, which suggest some directions in which the state of the art needs to be advanced. However, the language designer will need to be selective in view of the difficulty and cost of satisfying some of these requirements in the near future.

History objects retain data at various levels of granularity on the user's activities during previous and current sessions. This may serve widely varying purposes such as accounting by the system, recreation or modification of previously submitted commands by the user, or guidance to the help facilities.

2.6 Concurrency

Various kinds of concurrency are envisaged in the reference model. Concurrent execution of independent commands in different sessions requires no special provisions in the model, but dependencies between different sessions may arise due to concurrent attempts to operate on the same object in the BondedStore (see below). In this case, the designer of a specific language would need either to define individual potentially concurrent operations appropriately or to define a general-purpose synchronisation mechanism (or to use a combination of these approaches). A general-purpose approach is in any case required if the command and response language offers concurrency within a session, for example, processes with semaphores, message sending, monitors or pipes.

Some functional requirements and discussions of possible object types are included in the reference model, but, in view of the variety of approaches available, no detailed endorsement has been given to one approach in preference to the others, and this will be the choice of the individual designer.

2.7 Name Managers and Directories

Names are used in commands to refer to the objects which are the operands, and also to identify the command itself which is modelled as corresponding to an object representing an operation within the system.

Within the model, *Name* objects correspond to the external representations of names perceived by users. The *NameManager* defines the current name space by providing an ordered list of Directories to be searched, where each ElementaryContext in the current Context contributes a Directory to this list. The ResolveName operation on the NameManager will then try to resolve the Name via the first Directory and the other Directories reachable through it, and failing this will move to the next Directory on its list, and so forth.

A *Directory* object consists of a mapping from *SimpleNames* to *ObjectReferences*. Names may in general be composite, being formed from lists of SimpleNames. Name resolution then consists of finding the ObjectReference corresponding to the first SimpleName in the list. This must refer to another Directory if there are other SimpleNames in the list, in which case the remainder of the Name is resolved in this Directory.

2.8 Protectors and the Bonded Store

In a multi-user system, it is desirable to have protection mechanisms that are more refined than the mere binary alternative between ability and inability to resolve the name of a shared object. Therefore the reference model introduces the concepts of a *Protector*, and a *BondedStore* in which protected objects reside.

Objects of types defined in the reference model are considered to be "model objects", and do not reside in the BondedStore. For example, if a Helper is not directly accessible by name in a given command and response language, it could be considered as a meta-object introduced solely as a means of language definition in such a way that problems of sharing and protection do not have to be faced. However, objects which the language designer makes explicitly referenceable in a command and response language are termed "CRL objects", and these objects reside in the BondedStore. Their types are classified as *CRLTypes*, and these types can themselves be treated as objects. Many of the model types, such as Directory, may be selected by a designer to be explicitly referenceable, and thus are replaced by CRLTypes with similar definitions to the model types in a specific design. Other CRLTypes introduced by designers may bear no resemblance to model types, for example, CRLTypes corresponding to text editors, programming language compilers, or database systems.

Protection is based on a general model of *AccessRights* and *Permissions*. In order to access an object in the BondedStore, an Access operation is performed on the current Protector (i.e., the one in the current Context), passing it an ObjectReference and a set of Permissions. If the Permissions evaluate to a subset of the AccessRights associated with the object in the *ProtectionDomain* of this Protector, the desired CRLObject will be returned.

2.9 Constraints on the Initial State

Any command and response language based on this reference model and using a similar method of specification would need at some point to define any constraints on the state of the system for it to be a valid initial state for a user session. Some constraints concerning the objects defined by the reference model will now be indicated.

A CRLProcessor must initially be associated with the Transmitter at the access point of interest, and with a Context. This Context must contain references to a UserManager, a KnownUser, a Customiser, a Helper, a Protector, and a NameManager object which is a list of certain Directory objects. Each of these objects must be in a valid state—in particular, there must be objects in the BondedStore corresponding to all the ObjectReferences in a Directory.

Type objects for all of the above objects must exist, as must all types needed by these types and all operations defined in the interfaces of types.

An Activate operation must have been started on the CRLProcessor, and have reached the point where it has performed a TransferIn operation on the Transmitter and is waiting for the result.

3. Application of the Reference Model

3.1 Method

The reference model may serve as a guide at several stages in the design of a specific command and response language.

The designer might begin by considering the suggested functional requirements at the beginning of each of the following chapters. These requirements are not intended as either a lower or an upper bound for any language developed from the model, but are included as a useful checklist.

The next stage would be to examine the general structure of the abstract types in the model. They have been introduced as a suggested architectural framework for addressing the requirements, and the designer should informally consider how the types and operations could be extended and, if necessary, adapted to satisfy the requirements of a specific language. Simple extension of a type would consist in adding operations without affecting the semantics of existing operations, and extension of an operation would consist in adding parameters while preserving the original semantics of the operation when those parameters have certain defined values.

Another important aspect is to see how the abstract types of the model fit with the operating system on which the command and response language will be implemented. It is necessary to check whether some of the functionality required in the model already exists in the operating system, and whether the operating system primitives can support the functionality and the object types desired in the command and response language.

The most complete application of the model would then be to produce a full semantic specification of the language expressed in the style of this document, as an adaptation and completion of the definitions of abstract types and operations. The semantics of individual operations might be expressed in natural language, or using formal methods.

The implementor of a command and response language specified in this way could then

- implement each type as a generic module;

- design and implement the main program that generates and activates the modules and their operations. This main program, called the CRLProcessor, is the "driving engine" that reacts to user input by creating or deleting objects and by executing operations on the objects.

The model is not intended to be complete in the sense that all object types required for a specific language could be based solely on the types of the model. For some aspects, e.g. history and protection, it provides rather universal types which serve as tools for specifying the particular semantics wanted. That is, under the assumption of certain "natural" restrictions, all reasonable semantics could be specified by means of those types. For other aspects, e.g. concurrency, no such universal types were found adequate. Indeed, other specification techniques than the one used here have been introduced in the literature, and may be more useful.

The following two examples illustrate how the CRLProcessor for some hypothetical command and response language interacts with a user and with different model objects and CRL objects.

In the examples, we tacitly assume a human user is interacting with the system. However, the user might equally well be an application program, sending messages with requests for service to the Command and Response Language system, and receiving answers from that system. The main difference would be that the Transmitter would be replaced by another Transmitter geared to handle communication with the appropriate kind of application program, and that the Customiser would have to make appropriate transformations in order to communicate with a program instead of with a human user.

3.2 Example: Login Command

As an example, we consider a possible definition of the login command by which a user opens a session in a multi-user system. We assume that the system has already been started, which means that:

- a CRLProcessor has been associated with a Context, with Transmitter1, and (via the current ElementaryContext EC0) with Customiser0;

- the CRLProcessor has issued a DeriveCommand operation on Customiser0, which in turn has issued a TransferIn operation on Transmitter1, which makes this Transmitter wait for input (see Figure 3).

A successful login at access point 1 involves a sequence of actions:

1. The user (say User2, known to the system as Strauss) enters the command Login Strauss. Customiser0 knows that a password is needed as another operand of the Login. It uses Transmitter operations to prompt the user and to receive a password, say "Fledermaus".

2. Customiser0 returns the completed Login command in some canonical form Open(Strauss, Fledermaus) to the CRLProcessor, which activates its Login module.

3. The Login module calls the UserManager to search for Strauss among the KnownUsers and, when found, the attached UserProfile for Strauss is used to check the password.

4. From the UserProfile, the Login module gets the data necessary to build the Context for the user session. Execution of the ContextTree operation InsertContextTree appends one or more ElementaryContexts onto EC0, and EC2 is selected as the new current ElementaryContext; i.e., the CRLProcessor is now linked to EC2, and Customiser2 becomes the current Customiser.

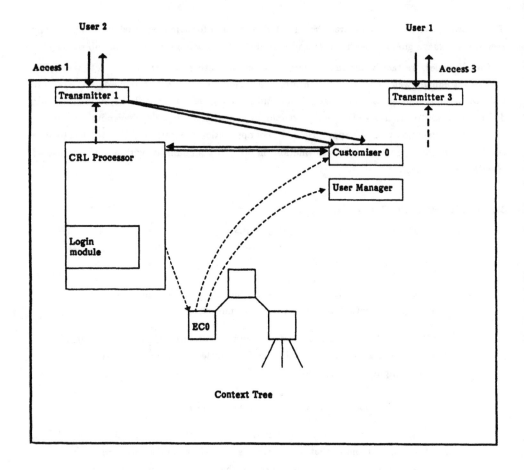

Figure 3. A system with two access points, where User1 is running a session through access point 3, and where access point 1 is ready for use.

5. The Login module sends an OK response to the CRLProcessor, which performs the operation CustomiseResponse (Customiser2, "OK", Transmitter1).

6. Now the user may issue commands that will be interpreted in his or her own Context.

The effect of the Login command on the state of the system is illustrated in Figure 4.

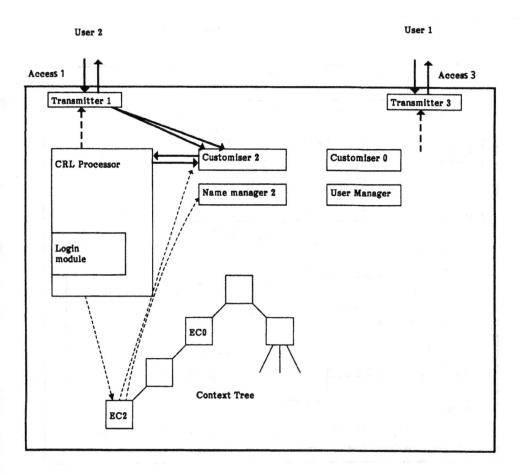

Figure 4. The Context Tree after a successful Login by User2 from access point 1.

3.3 Example: Copy Command

The following example shows how the execution of a simple "copy object" command could be defined.

1. We assume a CRLProcessor that uses a number of the reference model objects, and we assume that the user has already started a session and has established a current ElementaryContext with a current Customiser, Helper, etc., as described in the previous example (see Figure 5).

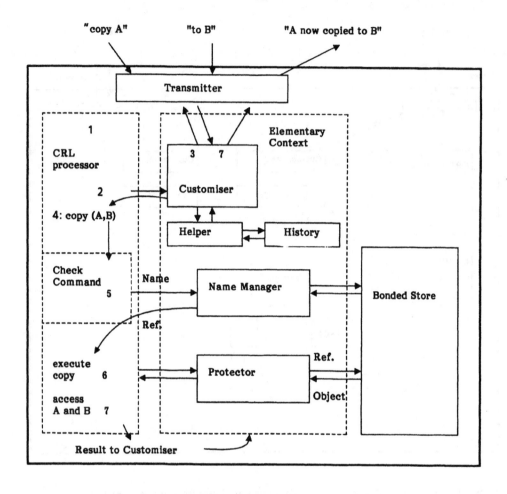

Figure 5. The execution of a simple Copy command in the user's Context. The numbers 1-7 show the sequence of actions.

2. The CRLProcessor issues a DeriveCommand operation on the Customiser, which in turn issues a TransferIn operation on the Transmitter.

3. The user enters the command "Copy A", e.g. by a combination of menu selection and typing at a terminal. The Customiser finds out that the command is incomplete and starts a dialogue with the user to obtain the missing copy parameter, say "to B". This may in turn involve operations on the current Helper and the History to learn how this user wants questions posed, answers given, etc.

4. The Customiser returns the complete command in some canonical form, say Copy(A, B), to the CRLProcessor which activates its Check Command module.

5. The Check Command module uses directory operations on the NameManager to resolve the names Copy, A, and B into ObjectReferences. The Directories are stored in the BondedStore which the NameManager accesses.

6. The CRLProcessor uses the current Protector to access the objects in question, i.e., the Copy program and objects A and B. At the same time, the user's access rights are checked. The user must have the necessary permission to execute Copy, read A and write B.

7. The CRLProcessor returns a response to the user. The response is handled by the Customiser, which shapes it according to this user's taste. Finally, the Customiser puts out the response, say "A now copied to B", by performing the TransferOut operation on the Transmitter.

In this example, the CRLProcessor accesses the Directories without protection (step 4). But the CRLProcessor could also be specified such that all accesses to the BondedStore pass through the Protector, and all the user's access rights are checked even before a Name is resolved into an ObjectReference.

4. Users

A command and response language exists to serve its community of users. It should aim to be as helpful as possible to the individual user, while protecting the rights of others. The detailed specification of the reference model begins by identifying some major requirements for both convenience and control of users, and defining some types of object which can be used to model the means of satisfying these requirements.

It is assumed that the system does not have direct perception of the *actual user* (person, program, or system), and the model therefore employs the concept of a *known user* to correspond to information the system has been given about a notional user. (Note that the concept of a known user is also used to handle the situation of an anonymous user, i.e., a user who is interacting with the system prior to identifying himself, herself, or itself.)

4.1 Functional Requirements

- The system description of a known user should be creatable, modifiable and deletable.

- An actual user at a given access point should correspond to a single known user at any given time, but may correspond to many different known users at different times or when using different access points.

- A known user may correspond to one or more actual users, including concurrent usage from multiple access points.

- User authentication should be possible before an actual user is accepted as corresponding to a particular known user. The model should support any authentication scheme, including none.

- It should be possible to dissociate an actual user from a known user.

- An actual user who has not been authenticated may be able to use the system, even if in a restricted way.

- A known user may be restricted to a specified set of commands.

- A known user may be restricted to a particular set of access points.

- A known user may be the registered holder of certain objects within the system (see the chapter on CRL Object Management).

- It should be possible to query past actions taken on behalf of a known user.

4.2 Overview

Commands and responses are modelled as entering and leaving a system via access points on the boundary of the system. Outside the system, an actual user is aware of some physical representation—usually visual, audible or tactile—which corresponds to what is modelled internally as a Message object. Each access point is modelled on the system side of the boundary by a Transmitter object. Input and output operations are defined on a Transmitter which will transfer information across the boundary of the system at that access point and map it between physical representations and Message objects. The Transmitter operations have no understanding of the semantics of the messages they are transferring and transforming. Such messages convey all input and output between the system and the user. A particular kind of Transmitter may represent an I/O device, a whole class of devices, or a network interface, and may thus resemble a "virtual terminal".

A Transmitter is associated in this reference model with a CRLProcessor which serves as the focal point for the processing of commands and responses for the current user of that access point. Each command and response is interpreted in a particular context, which can be modelled by associating the CRLProcessor with a current Context object.

Contexts form the subject of the next chapter. For present purposes, it is necessary to know only that via the current Context, it is possible to find the current UserManager object and the initial Customiser and Protector to be used. A given system may or may not choose to associate the same UserManager with every Context.

A UserManager refers to a KnownUserSet object which contains all the KnownUsers that this UserManager is aware of.

An individual KnownUser object models all information about a notional user that is persistent, in the sense that it is present in the system even when no actual user is associated with the particular KnownUser, and thus there is no interaction on behalf of that user. Therefore it is associated with UserIdentification, UserPass, UserVerificationCriteria, UserProfile and UserHistory objects. The first three of these are used to identify and authenticate an actual user as someone entitled to be regarded as that KnownUser. The UserProfile models all the information that is available to construct a suitable Context in which to start a session for that KnownUser. The UserHistory retains a cross-section of history relevant to the KnownUser.

A KnownUser object is also used to model the concept of an anonymous user. An anonymous user is associated with every access point which has been bound to a CRLProcessor and has no other associated user at a given time, so that a session will always be in progress at every such access point. A system may have different anonymous users associated with different access points.

Each anonymous user operates in a context which may for example limit the facilities of the system which are available—some systems may allow little beyond the ability to ask for help and to log in. On the other hand, systems which do not require logging in may offer their full capabilities to the anonymous user and operate entirely in this way.

Where the designer of a specific command and response language wishes to allow KnownUser objects to represent groups of actual users who may also be represented by individual KnownUser objects within the system, relationships and inheritance rules between KnownUser objects may be defined, but the reference model does not propose a particular scheme for this.

The CRLProcessor has one operation, Activate, which is the highest-level operation in the reference model, in that

- it could be invoked from parts of an operating system, not described in this model;

- all other operations within the reference model may be invoked, directly or indirectly, as part of the semantics of Activate.

The reference model indicates the approximate structure of the Activate operation, but some refinement of this would be at the discretion of the individual language designer. In the simplest case, there would be a loop over operations to request a Customiser to obtain input from the user via the Transmitter and transform it into a single Command. This would be checked and executed before producing a Response, which could then be transformed in the reverse direction via the Customiser which would produce an output at the Transmitter.

Customisers perform command and response tailoring. Customisation may depend on such parameters as user class, Transmitter type, choice of natural language, and terseness of commands and responses. The Customiser transforms Messages from the Transmitter into Commands in canonical form, and transforms the canonical form of Responses into Messages to be passed to the Transmitter.

One likely refinement is due to the fact that it is essential for the command language designer to define what is involved in checking command input, since this determines some of the response outputs which will be returned to the user. What responses are issued depends on the Context in which the command input was received. For example, the success or failure of a request to access an object will depend on the current rights the user has acquired with respect to this object.

The command language designer has a number of alternatives in specifying the component of the command and response language model which will perform the checks. One alternative is to fully derive the Command and then submit it to the Protector object for assessment, as above. Another alternative is to pass information about the command input to the Protector object as soon as it has been obtained, in order to start the checking at the earliest possible time. This second alternative does have the advantage of passing more semantic information about the command back to the Customiser to be used in the command derivation process, but it requires all commands to have the same structure, in order for the Protector to be able to perform checks based on the knowledge of the command structure. Note that the first alternative can be seen as a special case of the second one, with no interaction between the checking and the command derivation. The possibility of following the second approach in a design is indicated in the way the protection mechanism is defined. However, the actual use of incremental checks and the possibility of user interaction depends on the specific command language under design, and has therefore not been incorporated into the Customiser in the reference model.

4.3 Object Type: Transmitter

The Transmitter type of object is intended to be an abstraction of a basic input/output facility which is used by a command and response language, but is not under its control. Its operations may be used by model objects or CRL objects (see Chapter 10). Its operations may also be used by other objects involved in carrying out the operations on CRL objects.

```
TYPE    Transmitter
NEEDS TYPES    Message
DECLARE        m: Message
               t: Transmitter
INTERFACES     TransferIn (t) : Message
               TransferOut (t,m)
END Transmitter
```

Semantics

TransferIn waits (if necessary) for input at the Transmitter t, and then returns a Message.

TransferOut causes the Message m to be output from the Transmitter t.

4.4 Object Type: Message

The Message type is intended to correspond to a type of object which contains the information content of a message together with any auxiliary information appropriate to its external representation via a particular Transmitter.

4.5 Object Type: CRLProcessor

The CRLProcessor type provides for the control of the processing of commands and responses.

```
TYPE   CRLProcessor
NEEDS TYPES    Context, Transmitter, Command, Response
DECLARE        con: Context
               crlp: CRLProcessor
               t: Transmitter
INTERFACES     Activate (crlp, t, con)
END CRLProcessor
```

Semantics

The Activate operation would be used by an operating system to associate a CRLProcessor with a Transmitter and a Context and then start it running in a loop. (Termination would either be by an interrupt mechanism or by polling some object for a signal to terminate.)

Activate(crlp, t, con) thus performs a series of actions establishing the initial Context for a session. The actions may be expressed as the sequence:

CurrentElementaryContext := hd con ;
CurrentNameManager := GetNameManager(con) ;
CurrentTransmitter := t ;
CurrentCustomiser := GetCustomiser(CurrentElementaryContext) ;
CurrentHelper   := GetHelper(CurrentElementaryContext) ;
CurrentProtector := GetProtector(CurrentElementaryContext) ;
CurrentUserManager := GetUserManager(CurrentElementaryContext) ;
CurrentKnownUser := GetKnownUser(CurrentElementaryContext) ;

(Strictly speaking, this gives only references to the last five objects. In order to manipulate the objects, they must be retrieved from the BondedStore by the operation RetrieveObject.)

Having performed a sequence like this, Activate start crlp in a loop. In its simplest form, the body of the loop

- performs DeriveCommand on the current Customiser to obtain a Command in canonical form;

- checks the Command by using the Access operation of the current Protector on the ObjectReferences corresponding to the names in the command input;

- performs appropriate operations on command language objects or underlying system or user objects to execute the Command according to its semantics, and obtain a Response object;

- performs CustomiseResponse on the current Customiser to adapt the Response to the user and the access point, and cause it to be transmitted.

Thus it is the Customiser which is responsible for dealing with the Transmitter and with the individuality of the KnownUser, and the CRLProcessor is both device-independent and user-independent.

4.6 Object Type: Command

Instances of the Command type are canonical forms of commands, after the user inputs have been processed by the DeriveCommand operation of the Customiser. Essentially they should contain references (either names or object references) to a command and its operands. The details will depend on the design of a specific language.

4.7 Object Type: Response

Instances of the Response type are canonical forms of responses, as returned from the execution of the underlying command semantics before being passed to the CustomiseResponse on the Customiser to be adapted to a given user and access point. The content of a Response object would be information on the successful conclusion of a command, or an exception report on its execution. The details will depend on the design of a specific language.

4.8 Object Type: User Manager

Authentication of the qualifications of a user can take place for various reasons, including the starting of a new session, the resumption of a suspended session, and the switching of the current activity to a different one. In addition, a change in the user qualification can take place if either a different user obtains temporary access to the physical terminal, or the same user wishes to change his, her, or its qualification (in order, for instance, to acquire additional resources).

The effect of a successful authentication is to select a distinct Context and to switch to it from the current Context (the one in which the authentication phase was started).

The principal activities envisaged for the authentication phase are:

- identification and verification of the user

- selection of a UserProfile associated with that user

- establishment of the Context to which the switching will have to be performed if the authentication phase reaches positive verification of the user. The establishment of the Context takes place on the basis of the information associated with the UserProfile (possibly combined with some direct choices by the user). The Context could be a newly created one or the "resumption" of an already existing one.

- switching to the established context.

The way in which a "login" command could be modelled is that, like any input message, it would be interpreted within the current context. The first stage of interpretation would perform the FindKnownUser operation on the associated UserManager, and if this is successful and verification against some UserPass is required, this is checked by passing the UserPass input to the Verify operation on the KnownUser object. The UserProfile is then located and used in the context switching which follows (see the next chapter).

```
TYPE          UserManager  =  UserIdentification  →  KnownUser
NEEDS TYPES   KnownUser

              UserIdentification
```

```
DECLARE        ui : UserIdentification
               um : UserManager
INTERFACES     FindKnownUser(um,ui) : KnownUser
END UserManager
```

Semantics

FindKnownUser selects, from the UserManager um, the KnownUser corresponding to the given UserIdentification ui. An ErrorKnownUser is returned if um does not contain a matching Known-User. (Note that an apparently anonymous user is in fact represented by a KnownUser having a UserIdentification, although this identification might rarely be visible externally.)

4.9 Object Type: Known User

A KnownUser object serves to collect together the UserIdentification, UserVerificationCriteria, UserProfile and History objects for a known user. The first three of these subsidiary objects are largely concerned with the setting up of sessions with appropriate contexts for the user, while the usefulness of the History may include retrieval of previous command sequences to be reentered or edited, influence on the help facilities, and information about which sessions of a known user are still current.

```
TYPE           KnownUser :: History
                            UserProfile
                            UserVerificationCriteria
NEEDS TYPES    BOOL
               History
               UserPass
               UserProfile
               UserVerificationCriteria
DECLARE        ku : KnownUser
               upa: UserPass
INTERFACES     Verify(ku,upa) :  BOOL
END KnownUser
```

Semantics

The Verify operation checks a UserPass upa against the UserVerificationCriteria for the KnownUser ku.

4.10 Object Type: User Profile

A UserProfile object serves to represent information used to initialise the current Context for a user starting a new session. It is modelled as a reference to the Context the user wants as the initial Context, together with a list of input Messages representing actions which the user wants performed as the final stage of a successful login.

```
TYPE   UserProfile  ::   ContextReference
                         Message*
END UserProfile
```

(The term 'ContextReference' means an ObjectReference associated with a Context object.)

4.11 Object Type: User Identification

The UserIdentification type is not further defined in this document, although it might often consist merely of a String.

4.12 Object Type: User Pass

A UserPass might be a password string, a signature, a photograph or a thumbprint, for example. However, it is not further defined in this document.

4.13 Object Type: User Verification Criteria

The UserVerificationCriteria would determine when a Verify operation would accept a UserPass. This type is not further defined in this document.

5. Contexts

When informally describing the form and the semantics of a command and response language, the term context is used in many situations. Thus it seems meaningful and advisable to incorporate a formal context concept into the reference model.

5.1 Functional Requirements

The following list of requirements led to the concept of contexts. In this list, the term context itself is used in a rather inexact way, comprising the terms ElementaryContext, Context, as well as ContextTree, which are precisely defined in the following paragraph.

- It should be possible to make the semantics of a command dependent on the context in which it is executed.

- It should be possible to make the form of commands and responses dependent on the context in which they are provided. Thus a context may influence the customisation of the external representation of commands and responses, the nature of the help services available, etc.

- It should be possible to make name resolution dependent on the context in which it is performed. The context concept should provide for controlled extension of a given context, if an object is not found in the original context.

- By binding objects and operations to a context, it should be possible to limit accessibility to named objects and operations.

- It should be possible for a user to work in several contexts concurrently.

- It should be possible to hide irrelevant parts of the full system context from specific users, and to allow different users to have different, but possibly overlapping, system views.

- It should be possible to model shared objects (for different users or different processes) by overlapping contexts.

- It should be possible for a user to switch to a new context, or to return to the previous context.

- It should be possible to create, delete, and modify contexts explicitly.

- A user should be able to refer to specific contexts.

5.2 Overview

As far as a single user only is concerned, most of the functional requirements can be met by the concept of an ElementaryContext.

An ElementaryContext may contain references to

- a Directory (see chapter 11)

- a Customiser (see chapter 6)

- a Helper (see chapter 7)

- a Protector (see chapter 12)

- a UserManager (see chapter 4)

- a KnownUser (see chapter 4).

The Directory reference gives access to a Directory which defines the maximum set of named objects which are accessible directly (i.e. without explicit reference to an ElementaryContext) from that ElementaryContext. The objects themselves are not part of the ElementaryContext. Thus the rather static ElementaryContext is kept separate from the dynamically changing set of accessible objects.

All named CRLObjects have SimpleNames (see chapter 11). The command and response language has to provide mechanisms allowing

- users to structure the world of objects for themselves as well as for other users;

- the same object to have different SimpleNames;

- different objects to have the same SimpleName.

In the reference model, the Directory concept as well as the Context concept serve these purposes.

If two objects with the same SimpleName are referenced from different Directories with different SimpleNames, they can be distinguished by their different full names, each consisting of the SimpleName of the Directory and the SimpleName of the object. On the other hand, using Directories for structuring his or her world of objects, the user has to know exactly which Directories are referencing the object.

There are situations where the SimpleNames of Directories are not known to the user, e.g., Directories for local objects produced by nested procedure calls, or Directories for common objects provided by the system for several users. There are also situations where the user wants to access the "nearest" or "newest" object available, e.g., when providing his or her own version for a system utility, or when providing different versions of similar programs.

For these purposes, the reference model provides the concept of a Context, which is a list of ElementaryContexts. If the full name of an object cannot be resolved by using the Directory referenced in the first ElementaryContext, the Directory referenced in the next ElementaryContext is used for name resolution, etc. The list of Directory references of the corresponding list of ElementaryContexts is called a NameManager.

The Context concept explained so far allows the modelling of single user systems with no concurrent activities. It is mainly concerned with questions of visibility, nested name spaces, search strategies for objects, customisation, etc.

The concept has to be extended as soon as multi-user systems are to be modelled, providing object sharing, concurrency, protection, etc. This has led to the concept of ContextTrees. A ContextTree represents all Contexts in a complex multi-user system. It does not reflect the physical structure of the system, but models the way in which Contexts are overlapping.

The ContextTree is a tree of ElementaryContexts. Each branch is labelled with a Simple-Name, serving as the SimpleName for the target ElementaryContext as well as for the target (sub)ContextTree.

Thus, the type ContextTree can be defined as

```
TYPE ContextTree::ElementaryContext SimpleName  m →  ContextTree.
```

Figure 6 sketches the ContextTree for a complex system containing several networks. Each network contains several nodes, each of them containing several users, etc.

The terms network, node, user, etc., have been chosen only to give an illustration of a possible use of the abstract tree. They do not reflect any physical structure of the underlying network. Thus two real nodes of the same real network may belong to different network subtrees, etc.

The ContextTree u_{412} can be used to model a single-user system, whose user has no privileges to use or share other users' objects, but may work in different sessions concurrently.

The ContextTree n_{41} can be used to model a node of users who are sharing the objects of the node ElementaryContext n_{41}, and who may be allowed to use the objects of other users u_{41i} of the same node n_{41}. To further hide some of the users u_{41i} or to hide some of their objects, their Protectors or the Protector of node n_{41} may be used.

Finally, the full tree models the whole system and shows which Contexts or ElementaryContexts are shared by which networks, nodes, and users.

If a specific user may access arbitrary objects of the full system, he or she must be provided with the full information of the complete ContextTree.

The current ElementaryContext is the context in which the user actually works. The current Context is a list of ElementaryContexts. It starts with the current ElementaryContext, and ends with the ElementaryContext at the root of the maximal ContextTree visible to the user.

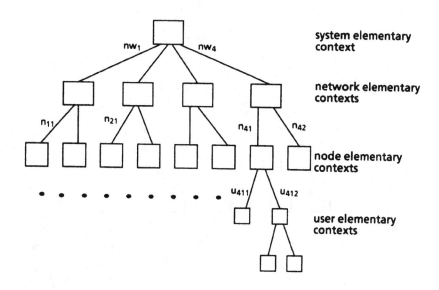

system elementary
context

network elementary
contexts

node elementary
contexts

user elementary
contexts

Figure 6. The Context Tree for a complex system containing several networks.

Usually subtrees or nodes of a tree are referenced by specifying a full access path from the root of the tree to the specific subtree. This implies that all subtrees of a given (sub)tree must have different SimpleNames. Thus a user may reference an arbitrary ElementaryContext or subtree within the tree visible to him or her, simply by specifying a full access path within his or her tree. This rule means some burden for the user if the tree is rather complex.

Thus in the following set of operations the rule 'nearest sibling/uncle/...next' is used. If the user specifies a relative context name, which is a list of simple context names, this name is resolved in that smallest subtree of the tree visible to the user which includes the user's current ElementaryContext, and which has a child whose SimpleName is the head of the relative context name. This rule on the one hand keeps to a minimum the information to be provided for referencing an ElementaryContext, and on the other hand it keeps name resolution for ElementaryContexts invariant against "remote" changes of the ContextTree.

Figure 7 shows how several ElementaryContexts can be referenced from a specific current ElementaryContext.

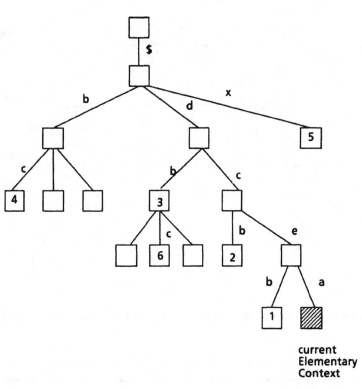

ElementaryContext	(relative)name	fullname
1	b	$.d.c.e.b
2	c.b	$.d.c.b
3	d.b	$.d.b
4	$.b.c	$.b.c
5	x	$.x
6	d.b.c	$.d.b.c

Figure 7. Referencing other ElementaryContexts from the current ElementaryContext.

Since a ContextTree is not static but is subject to dynamic growth or shrinkage, it is important to verify that name resolution remains invariant with respect to a wide class of changes in the shape of the tree. This in turn keeps name resolution for command language objects static as well.

In the following, we restrict our attention to a given single current Context. There are only two ways in which a ContextTree may grow: either the original tree becomes a subtree of another ContextTree (e.g., as a result of connecting a node to an existing network), or another ContextTree is inserted into the original tree.

In the first case, all objects and ElementaryContexts which could be accessed before the first tree changed can still be referenced by their old names after the tree has changed. The same is true for the second case if the the new tree is inserted at an ElementaryContext which does not belong to the current Context. If the new tree is inserted at an ElementaryContext which does belong to the current Context, the statement still holds for all subtrees of the new ContextTree which do not contain the inserted subtree.

A similar statement holds if a subtree of a given ContextTree is deleted: all objects which did not belong to the deleted subtree can still be referenced by their old names.

5.3 Object Type: Elementary Context

```
TYPE ElementaryContext:: s-Directory:    DirectoryReference
                         s-Customiser:   CustomiserReference
                         s-Helper:       HelperReference
                         s-Protector:    ProtectorReference
                         s-UserManager:  UserManagerReference
                         s-KnownUser:    KnownUserReference
END ElementaryContext
```

(Strictly speaking, all the references are just ObjectReferences, but instead of writing a well-formedness condition for ElementaryContext, we indicate the meaning through the naming of the ObjectReferences.)

Semantics

The interface contains only the default operations with the usual semantics.

5.4 Object Type: Context

```
TYPE Context = ElementaryContext*
NEEDS TYPES    NameManager, ElementaryContext
DECLARE        ctx: Context
INTERFACES     GetNameManager(ctx): NameManager
END Context
```

Semantics

GetNameManager takes a Context and returns the corresponding NameManager, which contains a list of ObjectReferences to Directories corresponding to the path of ElementaryContexts in the ContextTree. The NameManager defines the name space accessible from this ElementaryContext.

5.5 Object Type: ContextTree


```
TYPE ContextTree :: ElementaryContext
                    s-Subtrees :: SimpleName m → ContextTree
NEEDS TYPES    ElementaryContext, Name
DECLARE        ct,cto,ctn :  ContextTree
               ec :  ElementaryContext
               ecfn,cecfn,ecpn : Name
INTERFACES     GetContextTree(ct,ecfn) : ContextTree
               GetContext(ct,ecfn) : Context
               InsertContextTree(cto,ecfn,ctn) : ContextTree
               RemoveContextTree(ct,ecfn) : ContextTree
               ExpandContextName(ct,cecfn,ecpn) : Name
END ContextTree
```


Semantics

GetContextTree is given a ContextTree ct and the full Name of a (sub)ContextTree, and returns the (sub)ContextTree. If the full Name is an empty list, it returns ct itself.

GetContext is given a ContextTree ct and the full Name ecfn of a (sub)ContextTree, and returns, in reverse order, the list of ElementaryContexts along the path from the root of ct to the ElementaryContext specified by ecfn.

InsertContextTree adds a new pair [SimpleName → ContextTree] to a (sub)ContextTree, specified by its full Name in a given ContextTree. If the SimpleName is already contained in the ContextTree, the old pair is overridden by the new one.

RemoveContextTree removes a (sub)ContextTree from a given ContextTree.

ExpandContextName is given the full Name of an ElementaryContext, and expands the relative Name of another ElementaryContext into a full Name.

5.6 Examples and Extensions

In the following, some examples are given to show how the Context concept may be used in a specific CRL implementation. Further details can be found in the chapters on customisation, help, concurrency, and protection.

5.6.1 The Current Context

An operation is always executed in the current Context, whereas Names can either be resolved in the current Context, or in a Context specified explicitly.

The current Context may be switched either explicitly or implicitly, e.g., by the call of a CRL procedure.

A switch of Context may be performed by executing operations like:

    C1 := GetContext (ctree, newelemcont) ;
    Activate (crlproc, CurrentTransmitter, C1)

where newelemcont is the name of the desired new ElementaryContext, and ctree is the ContextTree within which we are working.

5.6.2 Particular Contexts

Before a user performs a Login operation, he or she may perform some operations in an initial Context without having been authenticated by the system, such as system query operations, mail operations, etc.

The Login operation may then either switch the user to a specific session Context or, if the verification is unacceptable, retain the initial Context as the current one.

Scope rules for local variables, produced by nested CRL procedure calls, can easily be modelled by the creation and deletion of ElementaryContexts, each of them giving access to local variables of the invoked procedure.

5.6.3 Searching

The ContextTree allows for modelling name resolution of incomplete Names as a search which propagates from a local ElementaryContext to more and more global ElementaryContexts until the Name is resolved or is known to be not resolvable.

Name resolution in complex library systems can easily be modelled by providing appropriate Name-Managers, which in turn are contained in their corresponding search Contexts.

As an example of how NameManagers (cf. Chapter 11) and the ContextTree can work together, we consider different users of the same project residing in different nodes. If they are maintaining a common project library, a corresponding library ElementaryContext should be located between each user and his or her node. This seems to conflict with the assumption that the users themselves are located in different nodes. But the problem can easily be solved in the following way: all project members get their individual library ElementaryContexts, referencing the same project library Directory (see Figure 8).

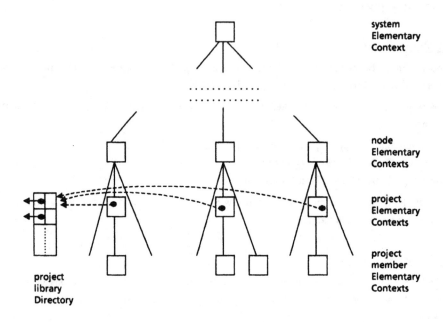

Figure 8. Sharing of a project library by project members in different nodes.

Thus the ContextTree may be used to reflect some gross aspects of structure, while refinements of this structure may be realised via appropriate components of ElementaryContexts.

5.7 Formal Interface Definitions

In the formal interface definitions a number of declarations are used:

```
ct   : ContextTree
cto  : old ContextTree
ctn  : new ContextTree
ctx  : Context
ecfn : full Name of an ElementaryContext
cecfn: full Name of the current ElementaryContext
ecrn : relative Name of an ElementaryContext
```

5.7.1 Context Operation: GetNameManager

```
GetNameManager(ctx) =
( len ctx = 0  ⟶  ErrorObjectReference,
  true  ⟶  ( ⟨ s-Directory(ctx_i) | 1 ≤ i ≤ len ctx ⟩ )
)
```

type: Context   ⟶   NameManager

5.7.2 ContextTree Operation: GetContextTree

```
2.    GetContextTree(ct,ecfn) =
2.1     ecfn = ⟨ ⟩  →  ct,
        true  →
2.2      ( let first = hd ecfn,
2.3             rest = tl ecfn,
2.4             ast = s-Subtrees(ct)
2.5       in  first ∈ dom ast → GetContextTree(ast(first),rest)
2.6             true → ErrorContextTree
         )
```

type: ContextTree Name   ⟶   ContextTree

Annotations:

2.1 If the full Name is empty, the given ContextTree itself is
    returned.

2.5 If the head of the full Name is the SimpleName of a subtree of
    the tree, the search continues with that subtree.

2.6 Otherwise it is an error.

5.7.3 ContextTree Operation:GetContext

```
3.      GetContext(ct,ecfn) =

3.1        ( let ast = s-Subtrees(ct),

3.2              ec  = s-ElementaryContext(ct)

3.3         in  ecfn = ⟨ ⟩   →    ⟨ec⟩

                true   →

3.4              ( let first =  hd ecfn,

3.5                    rest  =  tl ecfn,

3.6                 in  first ∈ dom ast →

                            ( let actx = GetContext(ast(first),rest)

3.7                       in  is-ErrorContext(actx)  →   ErrorContext

3.8                              true   →   actx ⁀ ⟨ec⟩

                            )

3.9                       true   →   ErrorContext

                    )

            )
```

type: ContextTree Name   ⟶   Context

Annotations:

3.3 If the full Name of the ElementaryContext is empty, a list consisting
of the root ElementaryContext is returned.

3.6 If the head of the full Name is the SimpleName of a subtree
of the tree, the ElementaryContext of the given tree is
concatenated with the Context of the subtree.

3.7 If something went wrong during Context construction, an
ErrorContext is returned.

5.7.4 ContextTree Operation: InsertContextTree

```
4.    InsertContextTree(cto,ecfn,ctn) =
4.1   (ecfn = ⟨ ⟩   →    ErrorContextTree,
       true   →
4.2      ( let first =  hd ecfn,
4.3            rest  =  tl ecfn,
4.4            ast   =  s-Subtrees(cto),
4.5            aec   =  s-ElementaryContext(cto)
4.6       in  rest = ⟨ ⟩   →  mk-ContextTree(aec,ast+[first → ctn]),
              ¬ first ∈  dom ast  →   ErrorContextTree,
              true   →
4.7             ( let act = InsertContextTree(ast(first),rest,ctn)
4.8               in   is-ContextTree(act)   →
                          mk-ContextTree(aec,ast+[first → act])
4.9                     true                 →    ErrorContextTree
              )
         )
      )
```

type: ContextTree Name   ⟶   ContextTree

Annotations:

4.1 As the last SimpleName in the full Name is the Name of the ContextTree to be inserted, it is an error if the full Name is empty.

4.6 The given new ContextTree becomes a subtree of the given original ContextTree.

4.8 The given new ContextTree is inserted into the appropriate subtree of the original ContextTree.

5.7.5 ContextTree Operation: RemoveContextTree

```
5.   RemoveContextTree(ct,ecfn) =
5.1    ( let ast = s-Subtrees(ct),
5.2          aec = s-ElementaryContext(ct)
5.3      in ecfn = ⟨ ⟩   →    Nil,
             true   →
5.4           ( let first =  hd ecfn,
5.5                  rest  =  tl ecfn
5.6            in ¬ first ∈ dom ast   →   ErrorContextTree,
5.7                 rest = ⟨ ⟩   →  mk-ContextTree(aec,ast−{first}),
                    true  →
5.8                   ( let act = RemoveContextTree(ast(first),rest)
5.9                     in is-ContextTree(act)  →
                             mk-ContextTree(aec,ast+[first →act])
5.10                        true  →    ErrorContextTree
                    )
              )
        )
```

```
type:  ContextTree  Name    ⟶    ContextTree
```

Annotations:

5.3 If the full Name of the ContextTree to be removed is empty, the result is Nil.

5.6 The head of the full Name must denote a subtree of the given ContextTree.

5.7 If the full Name is just a SimpleName, the corresponding subtree is removed from the ContextTree.

5.9 Otherwise the tree is removed within the subtree.

5.7.6 ContextTree Operation:ExpandContextName

6.   ExpandContextName(ct,cecfn,ecrn) =

6.1   (len cecfn = 0   →   ecrn

      len ecrn = 0   →   cecfn,

      true   →

6.2   (let m = {a | is-Name(a)   ∧

              len a ≤ len cecfn ∧

              (∀ i ∈ {1 : len a −1})(a_i = $cecfn_i$) ∧

              $a_{len\ a}$ = hd ecrn ∧

              is-ContextTree(GetContextTree(ct,a))}

6.3   in card m = 0   →   ErrorName,

          true   →

6.4   (let n = (Δb ∈m (∀a ∈m (len b ≥ len a)))

             ˆ tl ecrn

6.5   in is-ContextTree(GetContextTree(ct,n))   →   n

             true   →   ErrorName

)))

type: ContextTree Name Name   ⟶   Name

Annotations:

6.2 m contains all Names, which

  − map the first part of cecfn,

  − end with the first SimpleName of ecrn,

  − denote an ElementaryContext in ct.

6.4 The full Name of the ElementaryContext, denoted by the first
SimpleName of ecrn is the unique longest Name in m concatenated
with the tail of ecrn.

6.5 Check if the resulting Name denotes an ElementaryContext in ct.

6. Customisation

Customisation is modelled by defining a Customiser data type. The Customiser performs the transformation of user generated input (as delivered by the Transmitter) into sequences of commands, and the transformation of system generated response messages into output (via the Transmitter) to the user.

6.1 Functional Requirements

- Customisation should cater to special properties and capabilities of access points (as far as visible through the transmitter)

    - multiple I/O-devices;

    - windowing;

    - graphical input and output;

    - voice input and output;

    - input and output from and to programs.

- Customisation should cater to user preferences

    - syntax and vocabulary of commands (number and kind of operands, defaults, abbreviations, etc.);

    - form and vocabulary of responses (verbosity, representation, etc.).

- Customisation should support the capability of hiding details of how several primitive commands achieve a result, e.g. it could include

    - macro facilities;

    - translation from a nonprocedural language to a procedural one;

    - support of location and replication transparency of objects.

- Customisation should allow that a dialogue might be used to construct a single command, and that several responses generated by commands may result in a single response message to the user.

- Customisation should be context-dependent.

- It should be possible for the user to redefine the way customisation takes place.

6.2 Overview

Support for customisation is modelled by introducing a Customiser type of object, with operations DeriveCommand and CustomiseResponse. These operations, which are invoked from the CRLProcessor, may be considered approximately as having two steps. One step transforms the device-dependent representation of information; the other is language-dependent and translates between one command and response language and another (or to and from some internal representation).

Information representation concerns (besides device-dependent capabilities which have to be controlled via the Transmitter interface):

- transformation between voice input/output and commands and responses;

- transformation between graphical input/output and commands and responses;

- expansion of abbreviations allowed for input;

- conciseness of responses, help and prompt information;

- display of help and prompt information in menus or as a single message;

- optional redisplay of input information and optional demand of acknowledgement actions from the user (i.e., decomposition of human computer interactions for commands and responses into single steps).

Language translation concerns

- adaptation to users of different natural languages (e.g., replacement of vocabulary in commands and responses);

- expansion of default values for values of operands not explicitly specified by the user;

- expansion of command procedures when involved;

- expansion of "insert variables" in responses.

Transformation of input and output can be controlled by the user, mainly for influencing the way information is represented (e.g. demand for temporary guidance and then switching back to expert mode). It may also be controlled by the context, mainly for determining the richness and scope of the language currently valid for user interactions (e.g., switching to a very specialised database query language and excluding thereby all other kinds of inputs).

The ContextTree of ElementaryContexts (cf. Chapter 5) models in a straightforward way two mechanisms to support customisation:

1. According to visibility restrictions and the introduction of new name spaces (for operations and operands), new interfaces can be introduced (e.g., by mapping names of the new interface one-to-one to names of the old interface).

2. By additionally providing operations in an ElementaryContext which support many-to-many mappings for commands and responses (e.g., translate a single user action into a sequence of commands), rather general modifications of a user interface can be introduced.

More general aspects of customisation can be described in the model by introducing specific functions for customisation which are internally used by the operations, e.g., concerning device support issues. These functions may themselves be accessible via the described scheme of name resolution, and may thus be easily replaced by entering another ElementaryContext. This could be triggered by the user, or by the system if it tries to adapt to the behaviour of the user. For example, if the system realises that a user has problems in understanding and using the current interface, the system may switch the user to a more convenient ElementaryContext providing more sophisticated customisation and help facilities. All operations and operands accessible via the old interface may remain accessible via the new one.

Customisation can be seen as a programmable and/or data-driven facility with quasi-universal flexibility. The number of possible ways of interacting with the system for triggering the same effect may be large—depending on the number of different input modes and the number of different devices supported by the system. Also the number of different user command and response languages which are all mapped to the canonical internal command and response language of the system may be large. Conceptually there is no bound to introducing new external interfaces which the Customiser maps to the internal interface of the canonical internal command and response language of the system.

The feature of customisation may equally serve as a privileging mechanism— each user has only a language as powerful as needed— as well as a convenience function—each user has only to be as detailed as necessary for causing the required actions.

The functional power of customisation should, however, be applied very cautiously. Ambitious customisation is best regarded as a facility for long-term support of well-known demands of certain types of users, rather than as a means for changing interfaces very dynamically. In order to reduce potential damage resulting from interface changes, customisation should ideally guarantee a stable core of commands and responses, whatever alternative forms are offered.

6.3 Object Type: Customiser

The Customiser type of object has two considerable roles, corresponding to the DeriveCommand and CustomiseResponse operations.

```
TYPE        Customiser
NEEDS TYPES Transmitter, Command, Response
DECLARE     trans:  Transmitter
            cust: Customiser
```

```
                    resp: Response
INTERFACES  DeriveCommand (cust,trans): Command
            CustomiseResponse (cust,resp,trans)
END Customiser
```

Semantics

The DeriveCommand operation is a function which, when applied to a given Customiser cust and a Transmitter trans, returns a Command. The latter serves as a canonical form of a command which can then be executed. The general intention of this operation is that it should seek input by performing TransferIn(trans) as often as necessary, and possibly engaging in dialogue with the user by means of TransferOut also, in order to construct a valid Command. (If the input exceeds what is needed for a single Command, the surplus will be saved for the next invocation of DeriveCommand on the same operands.) The designer of a specific command and response language will determine whether DeriveCommand carries out any ResolveName operations on the NameManager and Access operations on the Protector in attempting to derive a valid Command.

The CustomiseResponse operation is passed a Response object, which is the normal result of invoking a Command. Its task is then to adapt this to the access point and the user, presenting an appropriate Message m to the user by performing TransferOut(trans,m). In the simplest case, the mapping is one-to-one between Responses and Messages, but in general it may be many-to-many. Moreover, some Responses may be completely suppressed and not result in any Message being sent to the user. In other cases, the Customiser may generate a Message for the user, even though an empty Response object had been passed to the Customiser.

In both of the above operations, the two aspects of customisation are handled by using knowledge of the particular Transmitter and of the user's Context.

7. Help

7.1 Functional Requirements

The requirements will be grouped under the general headings of comprehensiveness, consistency, appropriateness, and timeliness.

Comprehensiveness

Information on the following:

- how to obtain various forms of help;

- who I am speaking to, i.e. what object is carrying on the present dialogue;

- what other suspended dialogues is this dialogue within;

- what can be done next, e.g. available commands;

- details of individual command and response language commands;

  - syntax and parameters

  - semantics

  - examples

- other types of object in the system, including operations upon them;

- how to undo the effect of one or more commands;

- how to extricate oneself from a situation not well understood;

- how to do certain things not obviously recognisable from a list of command names;

- the means for users to help themselves, e.g. to issue commands of their own choosing after a command has been suspended for help, rather than being restricted to the built-in help facilities.

Consistency

The requirements here are for uniformity in:

- the means of seeking help;

- the presentation of information.

(These requirements are not meant to imply inflexibility, e.g., that the same request always receives the same response, but they require that there be certain general conventions and also general principles of flexibility which are applied to all types of object.)

Appropriateness

The help given should ideally be suited to both the individual user and to the situation of the moment, with the following characteristics:

- accuracy (obvious, but not easily maintained in an evolving system);

- direct, brief and friendly advice where possible, otherwise easy means of searching and browsing;

- controlled verbosity for basic help;

- different levels (including tutorial) for extended explanation;

- relevance to the context;

- ability to seek help about questions outside the current context;

- normal completion of help dialogue returns to the state in which help was sought;

- adaptability in the light of help previously given with the current command;

   - avoidance of looping on the same help message;

   - level of explanation;

   - order of enquiries;

- adaptability in the light of the session history of commands used and help requested;

- help based on an evolving model of the user's understanding and goals.

Timeliness

The temporal possibilities will be completely covered by considering the following phases of user activity:

- "between" commands, or, more strictly, before entering a command or after completing one;

- while constructing a command;

- during execution of a command (including its response).

7.2 Overview

The provision of help services falls into three main categories from the point of view of a command and response language model: those services intended to illuminate the user's problem-oriented situation, those which are solely concerned with the language itself, and those which are concerned with arbitrary facilities of a system which may be accessible through the language. With regard to the last category, a major practical consideration is that conventions need to be established within a system for the interface and semantics of the help operations to be provided by arbitrary types—the parameters to be accepted, and the results to be returned—and discipline needs to be enforced in implementation of the system to ensure that these operations are indeed supported.

In this reference model, we define a Helper type of object, and some operations associated with it. The most general operations are the emergency call SOS and the calmer Guidance request. SOS might for example be issued by a user who was totally confused, or had asynchronously interrupted some command which appeared to be doing the wrong thing or perhaps nothing at all. The intention of Guidance is that it should indicate the full range of sources of help, including manuals and human consultants as well as relevant commands such as those addressed to the Helper. This might correspond to a parameterless "Help" command, perhaps supported by a special key on a terminal or a touchtone phone.

The full details of each command, such as a general "Help" with parameters, are available from the Command operation which takes a given command name as parameter. An overview of all available commands is provided by the parameterless Commands operation. The operations Type(name) and Types are a similar pair giving information about types of object.

Since a major problem for users is often to map their task into the set of commands available, where the names of the commands may be a poor guide as to which are needed, another pair of operations Tasks and Task(title) are introduced. The title may be a single word or a longer descriptive phrase.

For information about the dynamic situation, Status is available, and for help in coping with the situation, Undo and WhatNext suggest how to go backwards or forwards.

7.3 Object Type: Helper

```
TYPE          Helper

NEEDS TYPES   String

DECLARE       name, title : String

INTERFACES    SOS

              Guidance

              Commands

              Command (name)

              Types
```

```
Type (name)
Tasks
Task (title)
Status
Undo
WhatNext
```

END Helper

Semantics

The operations on the Helper are defined to cause output to be sent directly to the Transmitter (possibly engaging in dialogue with the user) rather than returning results. Their output should be made as appropriate as possible by consulting the current Context and History objects, and should employ CustomiseResponse on the current Customiser to carry out the final adaptation to the user and access point.

The SOS operation responds with crucial status information and brief suggestions as to how to proceed forwards or backwards, and how to obtain more detailed help. It may also suspend any concurrent activities within the session pending the user's decision on how to proceed.

The Guidance operation responds with information about the on-line help facilities provided through the command and response language, and also how to obtain manuals, or tutorial materials, or human aid from system consultants.

The Commands operation lists the available commands, or at least indicates how a complete list can be found, perhaps by searching specified directories. Options might be available to scan the list in functional or other groupings as an alternative to alphabetical order, and a few words of explanation should accompany each command name.

The Command(name) operation produces information about the representation and semantics of the specified command. The information about representation will, by default, be appropriate to the current Customiser, but other options may be explicitly available. The information about semantics may emphasise aspects which appear to be relevant to the user's problems, as indicated by the current status of the session, or a history of similar situations and possible misunderstanding of previous help responses.

The Types operation lists the available types of object. Similar remarks to those for the Commands operation are applicable to Types also.

The Type(name) operation produces information about the definition of the specified type, and possibly about particular instances of it which exist within the system and how they may be accessed.

The Tasks operation responds with the titles of tasks about which the Helper can give information. A suitable form for this would, for example, be a KWIC (KeyWord In Context) listing.

The Task(title) operation clarifies the terminology of words used in the title, and explains how to carry out the task using the command and response language. Particular attention should be paid to distinguishing between apparently similar commands or ambiguous or frequently misunderstood command names.

The Status operation should supply information at various levels of granularity and system-dependence. At the language level, independent of the particular system, the stack (or tree in the case of concurrency) of current Contexts can be given to provide the gross status of a session. Within each Context, more detailed information can be supplied about the stack of currently active operations and their operands. In order to retain reasonable uniformity of a command and response language across different systems, the designer may allow language-dependent parameters to be specified on a "Help Status" command, but offer system-dependent information in response to prompting during the subsequent dialogue. The Status operation should also be able, by drawing upon the current History, to give historical information about how the user reached the present state.

The Undo operation advises on how to reverse the effects of previous commands. The extent to which this can be done will be system-dependent [9].

The WhatNext operation advises on what commands are usable in the current Context and with the given status of the system. This operation could be made sensitive to the user and the nature of the larger task that the user is apparently engaged in, so that its suggestions and reminders are usefully prioritised.

8. History History recording is needed whenever a user wishes to

- ask questions about events that occurred in the past;

- repeat sequences of operations performed before;

- return to an earlier state of the system by 'undoing' one or several operations (user-controlled recovery).

But a record of a user's past actions is also needed for a system to be able to respond 'intelligently' and to adapt to the user in a dialogue.

In this chapter we give some functional requirements for history recording and proceed to discuss a possible structuring of the history recording. If a system is to satisfy the functional requirements completely, all events and operations must be recorded. This may lead to an overwhelming amount of history data, and in an implementation one may choose to record only parts of the total history.

8.1 Functional Requirements

The functional requirements for history recording are that:

- It should be possible to trace a user's activities, including changes of context.

- It should be possible to record the history of operations on objects, such that answers can be given to enquiries about the events that lead to the current state of some object.

- It should make possible the tracing of parallel activities (by one user or by several users).

- It should support editing and 'redoing' of commands.

- It should support 'undoing' of commands and thereby allow user-controlled recovery to some extent. One form of recovery is to return to earlier states of objects.

- It should provide a tool for the help services, such that help may be given in an 'intelligent' way, reflecting the system's knowledge about a user's behaviour.

- It should support accounting and system administration.

8.2 Overview

Actions and events may occur either in sequence or in parallel, but for the user the interaction with the system may be regarded as a sequence of commands and responses. It is natural to think of such sequences as 'histories' and, as seen from the system, the totality of histories for all the users comprises the global history. In other words, history may denote collections of other histories and therefore describe inherently simultaneous or parallel events. In this sense, a history is like a musical score: each part is a sequential history but all the parts are tied together and synchronised, with the bars acting as time stamps.

When the entire processing is considered from the user's point of view, the single events to be recorded are input and execution of commands and output of responses. We therefore define a *single event* as a command or a response together with suitable data about the actual user and context. An *event* is a list of single events occurring simultaneously (or in parallel), and what we record in a *history* is a sequence of events equipped with time stamps. (The type Event does not occur in the formal specification because it is just a short name for a list of single events.)

Time stamps must be supplied by the CRLProcessor, the 'driving engine' of the model, and by choosing the time quantum the implementor may decide the coarseness of the recording.

If a detailed history is wanted (e.g., for system control purposes), one might define a single event as the call of an operation on an object. This would lead to a complete recording of all internal actions within the system, but we shall stay at the somewhat coarser level of user commands and responses.

The history may be organised in different ways serving different purposes:

- History collected per user and per session allows for accounting and user tracing.

- History collected per context allows for 'redoing' and 'undoing' of commands.

- History collected per CRL object allows for sharing of objects, tracing the development of objects, and user-controlled recovery of earlier instances of objects.

- Finally, the system may collect a complete history (the complete score) of all events for all users, to be used for statistics, accounting, and system recovery after failures.

This chapter describes only the object types available as tools to the implementor of a specific language. But it is recommended that a History instance be included together with each instance of

> ElementaryContext,
> KnownUser,
> each CRLType.

The data kept for each single event may be different for the different kinds of history (see below), but since the basic operations are the same in all cases we describe them all by means of one object type History.

8.3 Object Type: History

The object type History is modelled as a function mapping time stamps to events. This model ensures that simultaneous single events are lumped together into one event.

```
TYPE   History  =  TimeStamp m → SingleEvent⁺
NEEDS TYPES  SingleEvent
             TimeStamp
DECLARE      hist   : History
             event  : SingleEvent⁺
             single : SingleEvent
             ts     : TimeStamp
INTERFACES   AppendEvent(hist, ts, event)            : History
             RemoveEvent(hist, ts)                   : History
             AddSingleEvent(hist, ts, single)        : History
             RemoveSingleEvent(hist, ts, single)     : History
             SearchSingleEvent(hist, single)         : TimeStamp
             SelectEvent(hist, ts)                   : SingleEvent⁺
END History
```

Semantics

AppendEvent should be used by the CRLProcessor to append an event together with its time stamp to the current history. The operation adds the pair (ts, event) to the mapping of the given history. The time stamp must be found by the the CRLProcessor by performing the operation Time on the type TimeStamp.

RemoveEvent may be used to delete an event. The operation removes a pair (ts, event) from the given history mapping.

AddSingleEvent adds a single event to an already existing event with a given time stamp.

RemoveSingleEvent removes a single event from an event with a given time stamp. If the event consisted of the given single event only, it is removed from the mapping.

SearchSingleEvent searches through the domain of the given history mapping and returns the time stamp of the event containing the given single event. If the single event is not found, the result is the Nil time stamp.

SelectEvent returns the event corresponding to the given time stamp. If the time stamp is not found in the given history, the result is an empty list.

It may be useful further to introduce a chronological ordering according to the time stamps, and to have operations delivering the 'next' and 'previous' events.

8.4 Object Type: SingleEvent

A single event represents one system action as seen by the user, and the type SingleEvent is used to collect the information needed for history purposes. A SingleEvent instance may contain descriptions of

Command or Response that was executed.
Parameters and Results of the action.
The user and the session in question.
The current elementary context.
Completion time for the action.
Accounting information (resources used).

The extent of the data depends on the kind of history: in the history attached to a user profile the user description is omitted; in the history for an elementary context the context description is omitted, etc.

The basic operations on the type SingleEvent are operations to add, remove, and update data elements of the descriptions. The operations cannot be fully specified without defining more precisely the data structure of the single events.

8.5 Object Type: TimeStamp

The time stamps may be modelled as a set of integers with one operation Time which models the system function delivering real time:

```
TYPE TimeStamp = INTG
INTERFACES  Time()  : TimeStamp
END TimeStamp
```

9. Concurrency

9.1 Functional Requirements

- Concurrent execution of commands should be possible, as in

    - several local systems in a network,

    - a single local system with several users,

    - several tasks of a single user (including several subtasks of a single task).

- Concurrent operations on the same object should be possible.

- The user should be able to monitor the progress of computations.

- The user should be able to control concurrency by issuing

    - load distribution options,

    - scheduling and synchronisation rules,

    - execution sequence rules (between tasks, subtasks, operations),

    - starting and cancelling tasks (e.g. following a simple fork and join pattern, or more complicated ones which may be based on the notion of processes).

- The user should be able to organise cooperation between concurrent tasks, for example by:

    - message passing facilities (e.g. asynchronous, rendezvous, or synchronous communication; one-way or two-way communication; broadcast or not—the spectrum certainly includes mailboxes and pipes);

    - synchronisation facilities (e.g. monitors);

    - server disciplines.

- The management of integrity and recovery should be appropriate to concurrent tasks (for single objects, for several objects of a given type, across objects of several types). Different recovery strategies—e.g., dependent on the types of object involved—should be applicable.

9.2 Overview

Concurrency is dealt with by the reference model in two ways. First, different operations may be executed in different Contexts concurrently; second, this leads to the possibility that operations on the same object may be executed concurrently—as far as allowed by the object type and the protection scheme.

Concurrency which becomes visible to the user is related to different Contexts. The control and organisation of concurrency are achieved by means of (shared) objects of some special type which provides operations suitable for synchronisation or message exchange, etc. For example, a "monitor" can be modelled as an object with a very strict sequentiality constraint imposed on its operations; a pipe can be modelled by an object which allows writing by an operation within one Context, and concurrent reading by an operation within another Context, in such a way that the read may have to wait for the next write.

In this model, we consider name resolution to be completely independent from concurrency issues, i.e., the model has no notion of concurrent name resolution. Concurrency is considered only insofar as it refers to CRLType operations. Thus there may never be a conflict if operations which are resolved in the same ElementaryContext are executed by several Processes.

Contexts represent a sequential thread of operations. Thus one may consider a sequential process to be associated with a Context at any point in time. A language which provides Process as a CRLType has to map Processes to Contexts. A simple example of mapping Processes to Contexts is illustrated in Figure 9, where Processes are mapped only to leaves of the tree. The scheme of Processes derived from this mapping covers directly the forking or spawning of Processes (by splitting a leaf into two leaves which have the same ElementaryContext as father).

A nesting of non strictly sequential Processes is covered by a slightly different mapping: each ElementaryContext in the ContextTree may be associated with a Process of such a general type, and only the leaves are associated with sequential subprocesses.

There may also be a notion of processes which does not match the ContextTree in a regular way. For example, at different times the process may be associated with different Contexts which are not related to changes of the ContextTree (in fact the ContextTree may even remain unchanged).

Recovery for ensuring object integrity firstly concerns the types of objects which are used, secondly the way a Context is used. The kind and sequence of operations which are allowed have to be restricted, both for single objects and for Contexts. For example, starting with a BeginTransaction operation may be mandatory in order to have—associated with the Context—a Process which is well-formed with respect to recovery needs.

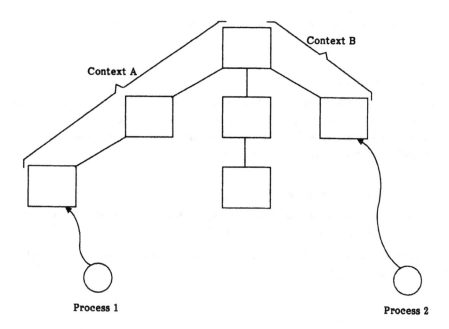

Figure 9. Tree of ElementaryContexts and associated Processes

9.3 Object Types for Synchronisation and Scheduling

Objects allowing for synchronisation and cooperation have to be introduced by the designer of a specific command and response language (cf. the mention of "Shared Access Control" in Section 10.3.2). In the case of a mailbox, synchronisation on letter objects may be accomplished by means of the operations SendMail, ReceiveMail and CheckMail. A ReceiveMail will wait until a letter object has become available via a SendMail from some other process. A CheckMail gives consistent responses on the status of the box regardless of ongoing SendMail and ReceiveMail operations.

Objects for synchronisation may or may not be explicitly created by the user. In the first case they may be created implicitly on creating a new Context to which a Process is associated (as the example of pipes shows), or they may be chosen implicitly (as the example of mailboxes shows).

9.4 Object Types for Resource Sharing

Resources are modelled as CRL-objects of special types which are sharable and which may provide operations (among others) for reservation, release and for choosing scheduling options.

Resource sharing usually concerns not only objects of a single type but objects of various different types. Thus provisions have to be made to cope with synchronisation problems across object types. The model allows for such provisions by introducing additional CRL-objects. The designer is free to introduce appropriate objects for governing interdependencies between different resource objects.

9.5 Object Types for Processes

Operations which allow the internal (e.g. Exit) and external (e.g. Cancel) control of processes have to be provided. They can be introduced by operations concerning a CRLType "Context", since processes are naturally given by Contexts. For example, cancelling an active process can be done by cancelling the ElementaryContext which is a leaf.

9.6 Object Types for Transaction Processing

Making a process well-formed with respect to recovery needs can be established by prescriptions concerning the Context with which the process is associated.

Synchronisation accomplished by "BeginTransaction" and "EndTransaction" can be modelled by introducing a Transaction type.

10. CRL Object Management

The command and response language user is ultimately interested in creating, retrieving, manipulating and deleting objects maintained on his or her behalf by the underlying system. Examples of such objects are programs, files, user-defined commands, etc. These objects are called the command and response language objects, *CRL Objects* for short, since they are the primary concern of the language user and can be directly manipulated by the user. They are described in the definition of the actual command language, and are manipulated by the commands the user issues. The class of objects used to describe the reference model itself are called *model objects*. This class of objects is used to provide a framework in which the semantics of a whole variety of command languages can be described, including the properties of the user-accessible (CRL) objects which will actually be included by a command language designer in a particular command and response language.

10.1 Functional Requirements

- Provision should be made for the storage, manipulation and retrieval of CRL objects.

- CRL objects may be persistent, sharable and concurrently accessible.

- The responsibility for the control and management of each CRL object should be allocated to a known user, called the *registered holder* of this object.

- The access to CRL objects should be dynamically controlled by the registered holders of these objects. As a corollary of this, it must be possible to control access to the outermost, the system, object.

- Accounting for system usage, and the management of system resources like space and time, should be supported.

The detailed requirements for the respective areas of identification of objects, their protection and their (shared) storage follow in subsequent chapters.

10.2 Overview

10.2.1 CRL and Model Types

It should be noted that model and CRL objects denote the dividing line between the reference model and the design of a particular command and response language. The CRL types are to be defined by the command language designer, and the designer may use the model objects to explain the properties of the CRL objects and other CRL concepts. Certain model objects will mostly be used to describe abstract concepts of the command language semantics, for example the BondedStore (see below); others may actually be included more or less directly in the command language by the designer, as already indicated in chapter 3. Note that the terms "user" and "model" may be dropped when no confusion can arise as to which view of an object is meant.

Each CRLType object defines, as one of the interfaces of the CRLType, a Create operation which produces an instance of the CRLType. Thus the relationship between the various types and objects in a particular command and response language system based on the reference model could be described hierarchically as shown in Figure 10.

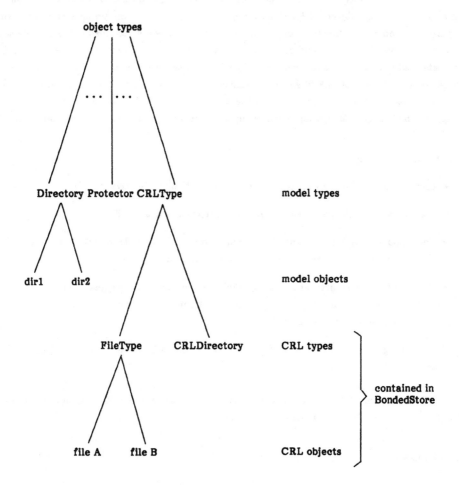

Figure 10. Objects in the Reference Model

The reference model includes a (model) object type, called the *BondedStore*, which is used to define the possibilities that exist for storing and accessing objects. An object of type BondedStore models the storage of all objects accessible to a command and response language user, irrespective of any logical and physical partitioning of the underlying system storage. The BondedStore is an abstract concept, and any structure a command language designer wants to put on accessing objects can be achieved by means of the Context concept and the protection and naming facilities. The BondedStore is thus very similar to the model of the store of programming language semantics.

The term "bonded" is introduced when referring to the storage model to emphasise that in general a system may be accessed by many different users, thus requiring strict management control on which objects may be manipulated by which user in which way. The CRL object management will make CRL objects available to a particular user only if certain levels of checking of the legality of the requested access have been completed successfully, i.e., the CRL object storage is not automatically open to the end-user. Chapters 12 and 13 will describe the Protector and the BondedStore respectively.

Another aspect that must be treated by CRL object management is the possibility of shared access to individual objects, i.e., the right of several users to manipulate or retrieve the same instance of an object. The effect of this on the object, and the ways in which such potentially concurrent accesses can be managed, obviously depends on the structure of the CRL object itself and the meaning of the operations applicable. When defining the corresponding CRL type, the command language designer therefore has to provide information about shared access protocols that will govern the access to CRL objects. The reference model can only go as far as offering a place-holder for such information; the implementor of the individual operations will then have to make sure that these actually behave according to the designer's specification.

10.2.2 Registered Holder

For each CRL object in the BondedStore, there is one KnownUser object, which is responsible for the CRL object and can allow or forbid other users shared access to this object. In an implementation of a command and response language system, this KnownUser, the *registered holder*, may also be the one to be charged by the system for the maintenance of the object, e.g. for its space consumption.

Note that KnownUser objects can also stand for groups of actual users, as already described in chapter 4. Registered holdership by groups of (actual) users may require protocols to establish whether granting certain rights to sharers is permissible.

Initially, that KnownUser object is termed to be the registered holder of a CRL object, which causes the creation of that object. Registered holdership can be *transferred* (see chapter 12), and with it all the rights to control access to the object. In a particular command language design, this can also mean the transfer of accounting liability. For the transferrer to transfer registered holdership means to cease being the registered holder. This ensures that for all CRL objects there is always exactly one registered holder.

10.2.3 Checking of Commands

The "bonding" of the shared storage is ensured by checking the user requested command derived by the Customiser and other objects for a number of conditions before actually performing the operation designated by the command. The protection of CRL objects from accidental damage or malicious interference is a concept that applies to many levels of object types and will accordingly have to be implemented at various levels of the command language system design. Examples are the initial authentication, repeated authentication, user interface tailoring, visibility control, etc.

In this and the following chapters, we are only concerned with those aspects of protection that relate to the management of those CRL objects which are designated by parts of the command derived by the Customiser on behalf of the user.

The exact nature of what checks are to be performed and how strictly the rules are to be applied depends on the particular command and response language to be designed. The object types defined by the reference model in the following sections are building blocks the designer can employ to define the central function of how a command needs to be checked before it can be executed. In particular, this means that only a subset of the concepts defined here or combinations thereof may need to be implemented, depending on how sophisticated are the requirements for protecting objects from unwarranted access.

As described in chapter 4, a command contains a sequence of references (either names or object references), the first of which identifies the operation requested. The remaining ones are assumed to identify the operands to that operation:

OperationName   OperandName$_1$

OperandName$_2$

. . .

OperandName$_n$

Note that all the operands and even the operation itself are CRL objects. They are protected by potential visibility restrictions and additional access control mechanisms, i.e., they cannot directly be retrieved from the BondedStore. The exact meaning of the command requested can be described as "Execute the operation object denoted by 'OperationName' using the objects denoted by 'OperandName$_1$' to 'OperandName$_n$' as operands". The checking of the command will now include all or some of the following:

(1) Check whether 'OperationName' denotes a CRL object that may be executed by this user.

(2) For each 'OperandName$_i$', check whether it denotes a CRL object which this user may pass to the operation object derived under (1) at the specified parameter position.

Note the similarity of the checks indicated under (1) and (2). If we view "execute" as an operation that may be performed on operation objects, then (1) is simply as special case of (2). We do, however, have to give "perform" a special meaning within the model, because otherwise the checking of whether "perform" should be possible on "execute" leads to an infinite regression.

As described previously in chapter 4, the CRLProcessor calls on the NameManager and Protector objects available, via the object denoting the current Context, in order to perform the checks indicated under (1) and (2) above. If an individual check is successful, the Protector retrieves the CRL object in question from the BondedStore. If some check is not successful, then a response indicating an error is returned. The complete command can be executed only if all individual checks are completed successfully.

Each of the checks involves two stages, visibility control and evaluation of permissions. Firstly, the CRLProcessor employs the NameManager of the current context to resolve the Name to an ObjectReference. Secondly, if the name resolution is successful, the CRLProcessor calls on the Protector to check whether the object denoted by the ObjectReference may actually be used as an operand to the operation specified. This includes "execute" in the case of operation objects.

The information whether a requested access is allowed is available through the Protector of the current Context. Chapter 12 on Protection describes the ways in which this information is created and how it can be manipulated. The control of visibility is dealt with in Chapter 11 on Naming, although those aspects of visibility which are relevant to sharing will require reference to chapter 12 also.

10.3 Object Type: CRL Type

10.3.1 Functional Requirements

- The model type CRLType should describe the class of all types available to a user of a command and response language, i.e., define what information is necessary to use and maintain a type.

- The model type CRLType should provide facilities to define new types and update existing ones by creating new instances of CRLType.

- Each object of model type CRLType should define a type available to a user of a command and response language.

- Each object of the command and response language available to the user should be an instance of such a CRLType.

- Each CRLType instance T (a *type object*) should contain information about the operations that may be applied by a user to the CRL object instances of this particular type.

- Each CRLType T should include at least an operation to create instances of T.

- Each CRLType T should contain information about what access rights are potentially available for such instances in order to enable the design of the protection schema and control the application of operations.

- Each CRLType T should contain information about the sequences in which operations may be performed on any object of that type.

- Each CRLType T should contain information about protocols governing the shared access to objects of that type.

10.3.2 Overview

Each model object is an instance of a model type of the reference model. Similarly, each object the user sees as part of the command and response language (a CRL object), is an instance of a CRL type, which defines the behaviour of the CRL object. Defining the behaviour of CRL objects means that the CRL type defines the operations provided for objects of that CRL type, the restrictions which apply to performing sequences of operations on any CRL object of that type, and that the CRL type defines all the information necessary to control shared, and possibly concurrent, access to any object of that CRL type.

CRL types may be defined fixed for a command and response language at the design stage, or they may be updated and augmented throughout the lifetime of the system, possibly by the end user directly. Unlike the definition of a programming language, the reference model can therefore not prescribe a particular minimal set of CRL types to be available to the user; it can only postulate that there will be CRL types, and that there must be ways of creating these, be it at the design and implementation stage only or later on as well. Therefore the reference model provides the model type *CRLType*, which has as instances (*model objects*) all command and response language types which the user sees. The CRL objects the user manipulates are instances of a CRL type, i.e., an object of (model) type CRLType. Note the similarity to the class concept of Simula, Smalltalk and other similar languages.

What CRL types will eventually be available to the user depends on the command and response language design. The CRL types may include commonly available command language objects like files, programs, etc., but they may also include abstractions of some model types, if the command and response language user needs to manipulate objects of these types directly. If the user is to be enabled to influence object identification by renaming or the introduction of new objects with new names, then the user will have to be provided with CRL types which define, for example, NameManagers and Directories. Some command and response languages may even allow the user to modify customisation or other predefined parts of the command and response system. In these cases, the CRL types will represent the user's view of some model types. They do not need to correspond to the model types completely, and in general they will be restrictions of model types.

Various objects in the reference model use and manipulate the CRL objects and therefore need the type information provided by the corresponding CRL object. In this way typing and protection can be enforced, as described in chapter 12.

In a particular command and response language it may be the case that the user is, for some CRL types, allowed to create instances of this type, while for others he or she may be not permitted to do so. Chapter 12 shows how this can be done by granting the user permission to execute Create on the appropriate CRLType object, or by forbidding this to be done.

Types in command and response languages do not have to be treated in the same static way as types are mostly treated in programming languages. Types may evolve, i.e., they may be modified for reasons of convenience or efficiency, e.g. by some system administrator. This modification may relate to part or all the information concerning the operations that may be applied to those CRL objects which are instances of this CRL type. In order to model the possibility that some users may have the ability to modify the CRL type definitions or introduce new ones, the objects of type CRLType will be held in the BondedStore, like all the other objects which can be manipulated through the command language.

Each CRLType contains the following information:

(1) Operations:

>   The operations that may be applied to an instance of this CRL type. This includes a specification of the operands of each operation. For each operand, the set of access rights required to be available for an actual parameter is specified. The operations themselves are described by their headers and the (partial) functions they perform. In order to facilitate managing this information, this part of a CRLType object will be described by a set of object references to operation objects.

(2) Principal Access Rights:

>   The set of access rights ("keys" and "locks") defined for this type. Subsets of this set can be associated with CRL object instances in order to indicate which form of manipulation is permissible. These access rights are referred to as the *actual access rights*. They are described by the permissions associated with the object in the appropriate protected domains (see chapter 12).

(3) Access Protocols:

>   The prescription of protocols for the operations on objects of this type. Operations on an instance may have to be applied in certain sequences to ensure consistency. This could, for instance, be specified by some form of path-expressions.

(4) Shared Access Control:

>   Information about shared access to operations, e.g., whether concurrent access is allowed, or whether mutual exclusion applies. In the case of concurrent access, locking schemes or similar conventions need to be defined. For example, operations could be grouped according to the number of concurrent executions which are permissible (see chapter 9 on Concurrency).

The information about a CRL type is used in the various phases of elaborating a command language request to invoke an operation on an object as described at the beginning of this chapter. After the request has been granted in principle, sharing and concurrent access have to be considered. Automatic delaying and queuing, as well as refusal to perform the operation, have to be modelled, and depend on the type (and thereby on what understanding should be given to the command and response language user).

The operations defined for object type CRLType include creation and deletion, as well as setting and retrieval operations for the various components. Update operations for the components are provided for reasons of convenience.

A command language designer may need to define relationships among the various CRLTypes, like being a subtype of another type, being coercible, etc. In order to give an indication of these possibilities, a type matching function is foreseen, which defines a set of CRL types, each of which is compatible with the CRL type being defined, i.e., objects of a compatible type can be used instead of objects of the type being defined as parameters to operations, etc. For reasons of simplicity, compatibility here assumes direct conversion to be possible. For any other form of type conversion, it is necessary to introduce special operations among the set of allowable operations.

```
TYPE CRLType

    1.       ::  s-Operations       : ObjectReference -set

    2.           s-PrincipalRights : AccessRight -set

NEEDS TYPES   BOOL

              ObjectReference

              AccessRight

              AccessRight -set

DECLARE       giventype     : CRLType

              op            : ObjectReference

              opset         : ObjectReference -set

              ar            : AccessRight

              arset         : AccessRight -set

INTERFACES

    3.           IncludeNewOperation (giventype, op)   : CRLType

                 IncludeNewAccessRight (giventype, ar)  :  CRLType

                 RemoveOperation (giventype, op)   : CRLType

                 RemoveAccessRight (giventype, ar)  :  CRLType

                 CompatibleTypes (giventype)   : CRLType -set

END CRLType
```

Annotations

1,2. Note that CRLType is not complete. More components would be
     introduced in the design of a particular command and response
     language.

1. Each ObjectReference in the set must refer to an object of type CRLOperation.
2. The access rights are represented by TOKENS, as defined in chapter 12.
3. The ObjectReference must denote an object of type CRLOperation.

Semantics

For a CRLType object to be wellformed, all the ObjectReferences in the s-Operations Component must denote CRL objects which stand for operations.

IncludeNewOperation updates a given CRLType by adding a new operation to its set of permissible actions. This operation allows CRLTypes to "evolve".

Since CRLTypes show an extensible nature and may allow new operations to be added, it may also be necessary to update the set of principal access rights (see chapter 12). The operation IncludeNewAccessRight adds a new access right token to the principal set.

Similarly, RemoveOperation and RemoveAccessRights modify a CRLType by removal.

The CompatibleTypes operation has been described above, just before the type definition, but will not be formally defined.

10.4 CRL Objects

The objects the user of a command and response language can directly manipulate are the *CRL objects*. They are instances of CRLTypes and are contained in the BondedStore, i.e., the storage and retrieval operations relative to the store can be applied. In order to deal with error situations, the reference model postulates the existence of a CRL object representing no meaningful information at all. This object is called the *Nil object*.

10.5 CRL Operations

There is at least the CRL type *CRLOperation* as an instance of CRLType. The operations on objects of this type include the fundamental operation "Perform" which is special in that it represents the mathematical idea of applying a function to its arguments.

The type CRLOperation needs to specify the protection (type and permissions, see chapter 12) required for each parameter to be passed to the operation. The protection specified will define what actions will be allowed to be performed inside the operation on that parameter. Actual parameters need to be of a matching type and provide at least the rights specified.

The type CRLOperation also needs to define how the context for the execution of operations is to be formed. Combinations of defining, calling and local context can be chosed by the command and response language designer.

10.6 Object Type: ObjectReference

Object references are the means by which CRL objects are identified. There is a unique object reference for each CRL object, which is associated with that object throughout the lifetime of the object.

The various phases of retrieval and storage of objects are linked by object references: naming returns an ObjectReference for a given name, protection uses this ObjectReference to determine legality of access, and, finally, ObjectReferences also facilitate the introduction of sharing into the storage model.

It should be noted that object references are a logical concept and not meant to suggest a pointer-oriented implementation. In systems basing protection mechanisms on cryptography, for instance, the object reference could be seen as the encrypted form of the information contained by the object, and the object itself as the decrypted form.

```
TYPE   ObjectReference

NEEDS TYPES    CRLType

DECLARE        objr : ObjectReference

INTERFACES     Create          :  ObjectReference

               GetType(objr)   :  CRLType

END  ObjectReference
```

Semantics

There is a Create operation for ObjectReferences, which will return a unique ObjectReference each time it is performed. Note that ObjectReferences are a concept of the reference model, and therefore do not require discussion of more implementation-oriented aspects, like finiteness of value domain, re-use of object references, etc.

The GetType operation takes an ObjectReference as parameter and returns the CRLType currently associated with the object in the BondedStore.

10.7 Formal Interface Definitions

The following declarations are used:

```
        giventype   :   CRLType
        op, or      :   ObjectReference
        ar          :   AccessRight
        store       :   BondedStore
        prot        :   Protector
```

10.7.1 Wellformedness Condition for CRL Type

```
is-wf-CRLType (giventype) =
1.    (∀ op ∈ GetOperations (giventype))
      (GetType(op) ∈ CompatibleTypes (CRLOperation))
```

```
type: CRLType   →   BOOL
```

Annotation

1. Each object reference contained in the operations set of a CRL type must denote an object of (CRL) type CRLOperation or of a CRL type which is compatible.

10.7.2 CRLType Operation: IncludeNewOperation

```
1.    IncludeNewOperation (giventype, op) =
          ( SetOperations (giventype,
                     GetOperations (giventype) ∪ {op}))
```

```
      type:  CRLType  ObjectReference   ⟶  CRLType
```

Annotation

1. The object reference must denote an object compatible to (CRL) type CRLOperation for the resulting type to fulfil the wellformedness condition.

10.7.3 CRLType Operation: IncludeNewAccessRight

```
IncludeNewAccessRight (giventype, ar) =
1. (SetPrincipalRights (giventype,
                     GetPrincipalRights (giventype)
                 ∪ {ar}))
```

type: CRLType AccessRight → CRLType

Annotation

1. The new access right 'ar' must not yet be defined for the type.

10.7.4 CRLType Operation: RemoveOperation

RemoveOperation (giventype, op) =
    (SetOperations (giventype,
              GetOperations (giventype) − {op}))

type: CRLType ObjectReference ⟶ CRLType

10.7.5 CRLType Operation: RemoveAccessRight

RemoveAccessRight (giventype, ar) =
   (SetPrincipalRights (giventype,
                  GetPrincipalRights (giventype)
                  − {ar}))

type: CRLType AccessRight → CRLType

10.7.6 Wellformedness Condition for ObjectReference

is-wf-ObjectReference (or) =
    (or ∈ dom store)

type: ObjectReference → BOOL

10.7.7 ObjectReference Operation: GetType

```
GetType (or) =
1.    (GetTypeInfo (RetrieveProtection (GetCurrentDomain(prot),or)))
```

```
type: ObjectReference   →   CRLType
```

Annotation

1. Note that the Protector 'prot' is accessible through the
   current Context. The protection information is associated
   with the ObjectReference in the current protection domain
   (see chapter 12).

11. Naming

As outlined in the previous chapter on CRL-object management, the BondedStore provides for storage, manipulation, and retrieval of user objects which may be persistent, sharable, and concurrently accessible. This chapter deals with how such objects are accessed. Users identify and access objects through names, and the chapter discusses how use of names should be managed and how Directories interact with the CurrentContext and with the BondedStore.

11.1 Functional Requirements

- It should be possible to refer to objects by names.

- Names should always be used within some context, and the same name may denote different objects in different contexts. However, there must exist a context in which the name is unique, i.e., a context in which the name denotes one object only.

- An object may have more than one name within a context, as well as when accessed through different contexts. Names may be simple (when objects are manipulated in a "local" environment) or composite (when used in a more "global" environment). The user should be able to switch context in order to change the "point of focus".

- An object may be renamed during the lifetime of the object.

- The naming scheme should allow for a name to denote an object residing in another system in a network.

- The naming scheme should allow for dynamic creation and dele' on of objects.

Other information about an object may be used to retrieve it, such as the type of the object or a predicate including one or more of the data values of the object. Such more general object retrieval schemes are not discussed further here.

11.2 Overview

The user addresses and manipulates objects through Names that are organised in Directories. The Directories available—at any moment—to the user are managed by a NameManager which defines the set of named objects visible to the user in the actual Context.

A Name is used to identify an object and consists of one or more components called identifiers. Often the identifiers are character strings (obeying some syntax rules). A Name may consist of one identifier only—called a SimpleName—or of a list of identifiers—a composite Name.

Names are associated with objects through Directories which are modelled as mappings from Names to ObjectReferences. The ObjectReferences in turn are mapped onto the objects themselves through the BondedStore. Within any one Directory, objects are identified by SimpleNames, but as a Name may refer to another Directory, an object may also be identified by a composite

Name corresponding to the search path leading to the wanted object by traversing several nested Directories.

The Directories are themselves objects kept in the BondedStore and therefore retrieved by their ObjectReferences.

Thus a Name is modelled as a list of SimpleNames. A Directory provides a mapping of Simple-Names to ObjectReferences, where any of the ObjectReferences may denote a "data-object" or another Directory.

This allows for modelling differently structured name spaces:

- A "flat" name space where all Names are simple and collected in one big Directory, on "one level" only.

- A tree of Directories where each sub-Directory contains a subset of ObjectReferences, disjoint from all other Directories on that level. There is exactly one access path to any object (or ObjectReference) from the root Directory.

- A net of Directories (still in one system) where there may be more than one access path to an object from the root.

- In a network of systems, a user on one system may have access to objects residing in other systems. This means that a Name may refer to another system, i.e., it is associated with the top level Directory of the other system. The occurrence of a reference to another system is tested during the name search operations and will incur activation of special network operations. These network operations are not formally defined here, because they are dependent on network and operating system structures and should adhere to relevant protocols, such as those of Open Systems Interconnection [1].

The basic operations on a Directory fall into two groups. Three operations perform the elementary manipulative functions find, insert, and remove an entry. Two operations GetSimpleNames and GetNames may be used to inspect Directories for purposes of more general browsing and management.

The user always works within a current Context which is a non-empty list of ElementaryContexts (see Chapter 5). Each ElementaryContext contains a reference to a Directory defining the name space of that ElementaryContext. The list of Directory references in the current Context defines the current NameManager, because this collection of Directories (and their sub-Directories) defines the total name/object space directly available to the user within the current Context. Whenever a new Context is "entered", the corresponding NameManager object is created and then becomes the current NameManager.

Objects outside the user's current name space may be indirectly available through explicit references to other ElementaryContexts (see Chapter 5).

When a user looks up a Name through the operation ResolveName, the NameManager Directories are searched in the order of the list elements, corresponding to a search in "wider and wider environments". The first reference in the NameManager list points to a Directory called the current Directory, which is the Directory associated with the current ElementaryContext. The last reference points to the Directory associated with the root of the user's ContextTree.

11.3 Object Type: Name

The type Name defines the set of quantities used to identify objects. A Name is defined as a list of SimpleNames.

```
TYPE   Name   =   SimpleName*
NEEDS TYPES     SimpleName
END Name
```

11.4 Object Type: SimpleName

The type SimpleName is considered as a primitive type. The structure of a SimpleName is not defined here, but is left open to be defined in a specific command and response language.

11.5 Object Type: NameManager

A NameManager contains a non-empty list of Directory references, and is used to resolve Names which may in general be composite. It is created as a by-product when entering a new Context.

```
TYPE   NameManager  =  ObjectReference⁺
NEEDS TYPES    ObjectReference
               Directory
               Name
               CRLObject
DECLARE        man   : NameManager
               n     : Name
INTERFACES     ResolveName(man, n) : ObjectReference⁺
               ListReferences(man) : ObjectReference⁺
END NameManager
```

Semantics

ResolveName returns a list with two ObjectReferences. The first list element is the ObjectReference associated with a given simple or composite Name. The second list element is a reference to that top level Directory in the NameManager, in which the Name is found. The Directories in the NameManager list are searched sequentially, and the operation returns the first association found.

ListReferences returns a list of all the Directory references in the NameManager.

11.6 Object Type: Directory

A Directory is used to store and retrieve CRLObjects identified by names.

```
TYPE Directory = SimpleName m →ObjectReference
NEEDS TYPES   ObjectReference
              SimpleName
              Name
              CRLObject
              BondedStore
DECLARE       dir      : Directory
              dirref   : ObjectReference
              oref     : ObjectReference
              n        : Name
              bondst   : BondedStore
INTERFACES    FindObjectRef  (dir, n)                  : ObjectReference
              InsertEntry    (bondst, dirref, n, oref) : BondedStore
              RemoveEntry    (bondst, dirref, n)       : BondedStore
              GetSimpleNames (dir)                      : SimpleName -set
              GetNames       (dir, oref)                : Name -set
END Directory
```

Semantics

FindObjectReference finds the ObjectReference associated with a given simple or composite Name in a given Directory. If the Name is composite, this requires a search through nested Directories, one level for each component of the Name.

InsertEntry adds a SimpleName and associated ObjectReference to a given Directory. If the given Name is composite, this also requires access to and insertion into nested Directories, one for each component of the Name.

RemoveEntry removes the association between a given Name and its ObjectReference from a given Directory. If the Name is composite, this requires access to nested Directories. If the operation removes the only (last) access path to an ObjectReference, the BondedStore management may remove the object itself.

GetSimpleNames returns the domain of a given Directory, i.e., the set of SimpleNames in the Directory.

GetNames finds all the composite or SimpleNames in a given Directory that are associated with a given ObjectReference. Each Name corresponds to an access path to the object in question. Often there will be only one such Name, but there may be more because of "aliasing".

11.7 Example

When a user issues a command like

"Put my work file into my Directory DATA under the Name PP.XX"

it may be transformed by the DeriveCommand operation on the Customiser into a canonical form like

STORE OBJECT oref WITH NAME oname IN DIRECTORY dirname

where oref, oname, and dirname are the actual parameters of the command.

In this case, we have:

    oref   points to the work file,
    oname   = PP.XX,
    dirname = DATA.

The transformed command, in turn, is executed as a sequence of basic NameManager and Directory operations as sketched below, where CurrentNameManager, CurrentCustomiser, ... denote the objects referred to in the user's current ElementaryContext:

```
(dirref, rootref) := ResolveName(CurrentNameManager, dirname) ;

IF  is-Nil(dirref)  THEN

  CustomiseResponse(CurrentCustomiser,

                      ⟨StoreObject, dirref=Nil, 'try other dir'⟩,

                      CurrentTransmitter)

ELSE

BEGIN

   ...

  dir := Access(CurrentProtector, dirref, writepermit) ;

  IF is-Nil(dir) THEN

  CustomiseResponse(CurrentCustomiser,

                      ⟨StoreObject, NOT write, 'try other dir'⟩,

                      CurrentTransmitter)

ELSE

  BS  :=  InsertEntry(BS, dirref, oname, oref) ;
```

. . .

END

The last imperative statement implies that InsertEntry performs a state change by directly altering a Directory object in the BondedStore BS.

11.8 Formal Interface Definitions

In the formal interface definitions a number of declarations are used:

```
man   : NameManager
dir    : Directory
dirref : ObjectReference
n     : Name
oref  : ObjectReference
bondst : BondedStore
```

In the definitions in this section, the operations access the BondedStore directly, circumventing the Protector. If protection should be enforced at all levels, use of the RetrieveObject operation could be replaced by Access via the current Protector; also the use of the StoreObject operation could be preceded by the proper check for write permission.

For a NameManager to be well-formed, all the references in the list must refer to objects of type Directory:

```
      is-wf-NameManager ( man ) =
1.       is-Directory( RetrieveObject( hd man ) )  ∧
2.       ( len(man) = 1  →  true,
3.          true              →  is-wf-NameManager( tl man )
         )


      type:   NameManager  ⟶  BOOL
```

Annotations:

1. The first item in the NameManager list must point to a Directory.

2. If there is more than 1 element,

3. then the tail of the list must be well-formed.

A Directory is well-formed only if it does not contain circular paths. This means that no Object-Reference in a Directory can be associated with a predecessor Directory of the Directory in question. (This condition is not formally specified.)

11.8.1 NameManager Operation: ResolveName

```
1.      ResolveName( man, n ) =
1.1       ( man = ⟨⟩      →    ⟨ Nil, Nil ⟩ ,
            true          →
1.2         ( let  curr = hd(man) ,
1.3                dir  = RetrieveObject( curr ) ,
1.4                objr = FindObjectRef( dir, n )
               in
1.5              is-Nil(objr)  →   ResolveName( tl(man), n ) ,
1.6              true          →   ⟨ objr, curr ⟩
              )
          )


      type:   NameManager Name   ⟶   ObjectReference⁺
```

Annotations

The operation searches through the Directories of the NameManager and returns references to the first occurrence of the given Name and to the Directory in which it was found.

1.1   If the list of Directories in the NameManager is empty, two
      Nil references are returned. This signals that the search
      has failed, and stops the recursion.
1.2-3 The Directory associated with the first reference in the
      NameManager list is retrieved from the BondedStore,
1.4   and the Name n is looked up in that Directory.
1.5   If the Name was not found in the first Directory, the search
      is restarted with the next item in the NameManager list.
1.6   If the Name was found, a pair of references is returned:
      the reference to the object and the reference to that Directory
      of the NameManager in which the Name was found.

11.8.2 NameManager Operation: ListReferences

```
2.      ListReferences( man ) =
2.1          ⟨ man_i | 1 ≤ i ≤ len(man) ⟩
```

```
        type:   NameManager ⟶ ObjectReference⁺
```

Annotation

2.1   Return a list of all the Directory references in the given
       NameManager.

11.8.3 Directory Operation: FindObjectRef

```
3.      FindObjectRef( dir, n ) =
3.1        ( let  first = hd n ,
3.2                rest  = tl n
              in
3.3            ¬ (first ∈ dom dir)  →  Nil,
3.4            rest = ⟨⟩            →  dir( n ) ,
              true    →
3.5               ( let  d1 = RetrieveObject( dir(first)  )
                      in
3.6                  ¬ is-Directory( d1 )  → ErrorObjectReference,
3.7                     true  →  FindObjectRef( d1, rest )
                  )
          )
```

```
        type:  Directory  Name  ⟶  ObjectReference
```

Annotations

3.1-2 The given Name is split into its head and tail.
3.3   If the first part of the Name is not in the Directory, the Nil object is returned.

3.4 If the Name is simple, the reference found is returned
immediately.

3.5 If the given Name is composite, the first part of the Name
is used to retrieve the first sub-Directory d1 from the
BondedStore.

3.6 The type of the retrieved object is checked.

3.7 The sub-Directory is searched (recursively) for the tail
part of the given Name.

11.8.4 Directory Operation: InsertEntry


```
4.      InsertEntry( bondst, dirref, n, oref ) =

4.1     ( let  first = hd n ,

4.2                rest  = tl n,

4.3                dir   = RetrieveObject( dirref )

        in

4.4         ¬ is-Directory( dir )  →  ErrorBondedStore,

4.5         rest = ⟨⟩

                   →  StoreObject(dirref, dir + [first →oref]) ,

4.6         ¬ (first ∈ dom dir)  →  ErrorBondedStore,

4.7             true    →  InsertEntry( bondst, dir(first), rest, oref )

        )


        type:  BondedStore  ObjectReference  Name  ObjectReference
                       ⟶  BondedStore
```

Annotations

4.1-2 The given Name is split into its first component and the rest.

4.3 The Directory object is retrieved from the BondedStore.

4.4 The type of the Directory object is checked.

4.5 If the given Name is simple, the Directory is updated
and put back into the BondedStore.

4.6 The given Name is composite, and its first part must belong
to the domain of the Directory.

4.7 A recursion is started, where the last part of the Name is
searched for in the sub-Directory denoted by the head of the Name.

11.8.5 Directory Operation: RemoveEntry

```
5.      RemoveEntry( bondst, dirref, n ) =

5.1        ( let  first = hd n ,

5.2               rest  = tl n ,

5.3               dir   = RetrieveObject( dirref )

         in

5.4            ¬ is-Directory( dir )      →  ErrorBondedStore,

5.5            ¬ (first ∈ dom dir)        →  ErrorBondedStore,

5.6            rest = ⟨⟩  →  StoreObject(dirref, dir - {first}) ,

5.7            true       →  RemoveEntry( bondst, dir(first), rest )

         )


        type:   BondedStore  ObjectReference  Name  ⟶  BondedStore
```

Annotations

5.1-3 Split the given Name into its first component and the rest,
       and retrieve the Directory object from the BondedStore.
5.4   The object must be of type Directory.
5.5   The first part of the Name must belong to the domain of the
       Directory.
5.6   If the Name is simple, the Directory is updated and put back
       into the BondedStore.
5.7   The given Name is composite, and a recursive search is
       started in the sub-Directory denoted by the first part of
       the Name.

11.8.6 Directory Operation: GetSimpleNames

```
6.      GetSimpleNames( dir ) =   dom dir


        type:   Directory  ⟶  SimpleName -set
```

Annotation

6.   The operation returns the set of SimpleNames in the
     domain of the given Directory.

11.8.7 Directory Operation: GetNames

7.   GetNames(dir, oref) =

7.1   { n | FindObjectRef(dir, n) = oref }

       type: Directory ObjectReference $\longrightarrow$ Name -set

Annotation

7.1   The operation finds all the access paths in the given
      Directory to the given ObjectReference oref. The result
      is returned as the set of simple or composite Names that
      are associated with oref.

12. Protection

12.1 Functional Requirements

- Users may perform only those operations on CRL objects which the designer has provided when defining that CRL type of which the objects are instances.

- The creator of a CRL object should be able to determine which of the operations defined by the CRL type should initially be applicable to the object created.

- The known user who creates the object should be the initial registered holder.

- The registered holder of an object may transfer ownership to another known user.

- The owner of an object should be able to allow other known users to become sharers, i.e., be able to perform certain operations on that object by being granted certain forms of access.

- It should be possible to attach certain conditions to the accesses granted. These conditions should allow the actual right to perform a particular operation to be determined depending on the context in which the sharer tries to exercise the granted access.

- The registered holder of an object shall be able to revoke access granted to sharers partially or completely.

- A known user cannot perform an operation on an object unless he or she is a registered holder or a sharer of the object, and unless, in the context of requesting the operation, the known user has the right to perform the operation on that object.

- It should be possible to specify defaults, which are to be used for granting permissions to certain sharers whenever an object is created.

- The specification of defaults should be context-dependent.

- Both coarser (groups of operations) and finer (constraints on passing objects as certain parameters) granularity of protection should be provided.

- The form of protection scheme applied may depend on the context.

12.2 Overview

The protection model is based on the idea that every object is held in the single BondedStore, with access controlled by the Protector of the current context.

Any attempt to access an object is checked against *AccessRights* which are currently held by the issuer of the request. Each operation which may be invoked specifies what Access Rights are required for parameters in order for the operation to function properly.

The possible Access Rights which can be held or required for an object may depend on the (CRL) type of that object.

In order to express that rights held for accessing an object may depend on the current context in which the right is going to be exercised, the notion of *Permissions* is introduced. Permissions can be viewed as conditional Access Rights. Upon elaboration of an operation invocation, the Permissions held by the invoker are evaluated in the current context. This process will return AccessRights. This allows a dependency on time, space and other conditions.

For example, a Permission

IF time > 5pm THEN {RightToBackUpAccounts} END IF

would return the (singleton) set of Access Rights

{RightToBackUpAccounts}

only IF it is later than 5 o'clock in the evening, and the empty set of AccessRights otherwise.

The rights required by an operation may also depend on the context, for instance to allow a security classification scheme to be implemented. Parameter specifications in operations therefore also include Permissions, rather than AccessRights directly. Thus one can foresee a symmetric use of Permissions by, for example, specifying

IF LastSecurityClass = Unclassified THEN {RighttoBroadcast} END IF

as a Permission required for an actual operand of an operation. This would state that the set of currently available rights on the operand must include the right to publicly broadcast the information if the information last processed by this operation was unclassified .

At invocation both the required and the possessed Permissions are evaluated and the resulting sets of AccessRights are compared. Access is granted only if the possessed AccessRights form a superset of the required ones.

12.3 Object Type: Protector

Protection information is associated with ObjectReferences. (ObjectReferences are returned as part of the object identification described in chapter 11.) The mappings from ObjectReferences to protection information are contained in objects of (model) type *ProtectionDomain*. Being a mapping, a ProtectionDomain can contain a particular ObjectReference only once in its domain of definition. Protection levels may be changed by changing the current ProtectionDomain to be used in checking the legality of accesses. A set of such ProtectionDomains is provided in PROTECTOR objects. Every Protector object also identifies a home and a current ProtectionDomain among the elements of the set of ProtectionDomains. The home domain is the default when the user connects to the system, and the current one is the one the user last switched to.

There is a Protector object identified by each ElementaryContext, making a Protector available implicitly at any time and allowing protection to be dependent on the current context.

Whereas the NameManager contains a *list* of Directories to allow for search lists, the Protector consists of a *set* of ProtectionDomains, since there cannot be an automatic search for the required rights if a rigid access control is to be maintained. Different policies can be implemented using the primitives defined here.

The main operation on Protector objects is Access, which is invoked by the CRLProcessor and is passed an ObjectReference and a set of Permissions. If the Permissions evaluate to a set of AccessRights which constitutes a subset of those associated (dynamically, by means of Permissions) with the ObjectReference in the current ProtectionDomain, then the Protector retrieves the object from the BondedStore and returns it. Otherwise an error is indicated.

```
TYPE Protector  ::   s-HomeDomain       :  ProtectionDomain
                     s-CurrentDomain    :  ProtectionDomain
                     s-DomainSet        :  ProtectionDomain -set
NEEDS TYPES   ProtectionDomain
              ObjectReference
              BondedStore
              CRLObject
              Protection
DECLARE       prot  :  Protector
              pdom  :  ProtectionDomain
              objref:  ObjectReference
              obj   :  CRLObject
              reqp  :  Protection
INTERFACES
              Access (prot, objref, reqp)   :  CRLObject
              AddProtectionDomain (prot, pdom),
              RemoveProtectionDomain (prot, pdom) : Protector
END Protector
```

Semantics

All protectors must fulfill the condition that the home and current ProtectionDomains (which may coincide) are contained in the set of ProtectionDomains. Furthermore, all the ProtectionDomains must be wellformed.

Note that Access may return a Nil object, if the access required was not considered legal.

The Access operation takes a Protector, an ObjectReference and a Protection object as parameters. The Protection object specifies which type and protection are required by the operation the issuer of the Access operation wants to execute. If the Protector associates Protection information with the ObjectReference such that the requested access would be legal, then the object denoted by ObjectReference is retrieved from the BondedStore. Otherwise a Nil object is returned.

AddProtectionDomain enlarges the set of ProtectionDomain by the one given.

RemoveProtectionDomain removes the ProtectionDomain passed as a parameter from the set of domains, thus reducing the possible levels of protection. Note that neither the current nor the home ProtectionDomain may be removed without violating the wellformedness condition of the Protector object.

12.4 Object Type : ProtectionDomain

A *ProtectionDomain* defines a mapping from a set of ObjectReferences to a set of Protection objects. Using the Protection operation, the current Protection associated with an ObjectReference can be retrieved for checking.

```
TYPE ProtectionDomain = ObjectReference  m → Protection

NEED TYPES   ObjectReference

             Protection

             Permission

DECLARE      pdom  :  ProtectionDomain

             objref:  ObjectReference

             p     :  Protection

             perm  :  Permission

INTERFACES   Add ProtectedObject (pdom, objref, p),

             Remove ProtectedObject (pdom, objref),

             Allow (pdom, objref, perm),

             Disallow (pdom, objref, perm)       :  ProtectionDomain

             RetrieveProtection (pdom, objref)  :  Protection

END ProtectionDomain
```

Semantics

For all ObjectReferences contained in the domain of a ProtectionDomain object, it must hold that the Object Reference is wellformed, i.e., contained in the domain of the BondedStore, and that the Protection the ObjectReference maps to under the ProtectionDomain is wellformed.

AddProtectedObject enlarges a given ProtectionDomain by adding another ObjectReference - Protection pair. If the ObjectReference is already contained in the ProtectionDomain, then the new Protection supersedes the old one.

RemoveProtectedObject removes an ObjectReference with its associated Protection from the ProtectionDomain specified. As a result, *no* operation is allowed on the object denoted by the ObjectReference while the ProtectionDomain is the current one.

The Allow operation adds a new Permission to the Protection associated with the ObjectReference given. Since legality checks are based on sets of AccessRights, it does not matter whether Permissions (and thereby the consistent AccessRights) are already specified. The Permission must be consistent with the type of object.

The Disallow operation removes a Permission from the given Protection of a given ObjectReference in a given ProtectionDomain. The Permission must be consistent with the type of object. If that is not the case or the Permission is not wellformed, then the ProtectedDomain remains unchanged and an appropriate response is generated.

RetrieveProtection uses the mapping property of Protection Domains to retrieve the Protection object associated with an Object Reference in a ProtectionDomain.

12.5 Object Type : Protection

The protection mechanism allows for coarser protection on the basis of groups of operations, as well as dynamic, individual checking of objects passed to certain parameter positions. The first is related to type checking in programming languages, whereas the latter one is access control proper.

Therefore the Protection objects associated with ObjectReferences through ProtectionDomains contain two components, one describing the objects CRLType, and the other the set of Permissions associated with it.

```
TYPE Protection        s-TypeInfo   : CRLType
                       s-Permissions: Permission -set
NEEDS TYPES            BOOL
                       CRLType
                       Permission
DECLARE                givenp, reqdp : Protection
INTERFACE              IsAllowedUse (givenp, reqdp) : BOOL
END Protection
```

Semantics

All Permissions contained in the set in a Protection must be wellformed with respect to the type given, i.e. they must always evaluate to a set of AccessRights which is a subset of the set of principal rights defined for that CRLType.

IsAllowedUse evaluates both the given and the required Permission in the current context and then checks whether the resulting set of required AccessRights is a subset of those AccessRights actually given in the current ProtectionDomain.

A command language designer may want to change this simple subscribing relationship into a more elaborate scheme.

12.6 Object Type: Permission

The concept of Permission allows rights to be context-dependent. Permissions are allowed and forbidden for users on their objects, and granted to or revoked from other users. Permissions need to be evaluated to yield sets of AccessRights.

There are broadly two classes of Permissions:

unconditional Permissions, which always return the same set of AccessRights when evaluated.

conditional Permissions, which may return different sets of AccessRights depending on some conditions.

A conditional Permission could, for example, be specified as something like

IF NoOfUsers < 2 THEN {HaltSys, Reboot} ELSE {CloseLogin} END IF

which would allow the system to be stopped only if there were not too many other users on the system. The exact details of what can be used in a condition to a Permission obviously depends on the specific command and response language to be designed.

It should be noted that unconditional Permissions are a special case of conditional Permissions, having true as the condition. We therefore specify the more general form only, although command language designers may choose to offer two syntactically different options.

```
TYPE  Permission    s-PermCondition : ControlExpression

                    s-ThenRights    : AccessRight -set

                    s-ElseRights    : AccessRight -set

NEEDS TYPES         ControlExpression, AccessRight,  BOOL

DECLARE             perm : Permission

INTERFACE           EvaluatePermission (perm) : AccessRight -set

END Permission
```

Semantics

The Permissions must be wellformed with respect to that particular CRLType in connection with
which they are to be used in Protection objects. This means that the two sets of AccessRights
must form subsets of the set of principal AccessRights of that CRLType.

EvaluatePermission takes a Permission, and evaluates the condition contained in it in the current
context (which is implicitly available). Depending on whether the condition turns out to be true
or False, it returns the set of AccessRights specified in the ThenRights or that specified in the
ElseRights component. Note that this operation is one which the command language designer will
most likely want to elaborate on.

12.7 Object Type: Access Right

This object type allows for the construction of the basic tokens that are used in the CRLType
definitions to denote rights. AccessRights are based on the type Token, which is predefined in
VDM and introduces a potentially infinite set of distinct, elementary objects. They act like literals
in enumeration types in programming languages.

Besides these primitive AccessRights, additional rights are needed to control the granting and
transferring of rights. The operations RightToGrant and RightToTransfer serve these purposes.
Some of these continuations may not be meaningful in a particular command language, and the
designer can modify or remove these accordingly.

```
TYPE AccessRight
NEEDS TYPES   TOKEN
DECLARE       t: TOKEN
              ar: AccessRight
INTERFACES    IntroduceAccessRight (t),
              RightToGrant (ar),
              RightToTransfer (ar) : AccessRight
END AccessRight
```

Semantics

IntroduceAccessRight allows a token to be used as an AccessRight.

RightToGrant produces an AccessRight controlling the legality of granting the right passed as
parameter to other users. A command language designer could elaborate on this by introducing
an additional parameter which would restrict the right to grant to certain classes of users.

RightToTransfer provides an AccessRight controlling the legality of transferring the right passed
as parameter to other users. A command language designer could elaborate on this by introducing
an additional parameter which would restrict the right to transfer to certain classes of users.

12.8 Object Type: Control Expression

This type is a placeholder for the command and response language designer to define the conditions which should be allowed to control permissions.

```
TYPE ControlExpression

NEEDS TYPES    BOOL

DECLARE        ce : Control Expression

INTERFACE      Evaluate ControlExpression (ce) : BOOL

END  ControlExpression
```

Semantics

EvaluateControlExpression uses the current context, which is available implicitly, to determine the value of the parameter passed to it.

12.9 Formal Interface Definitions

The following declarations are used:

> prot : Protector
> pdom : ProtectionDomain
> bs : BondedStore
> objref: ObjectReference
> givenp, p, reqp: Protection
> perm : Permission
> t : CRLType

12.9.1 Wellformedness Condition for Protector

> is-wf-Protector (prot)   =
>
> > (∀ pdom ∈ GetDomainSet (prot))
> >
> > > (is-wf-ProtectionDomain(pdom))
> >
> > ∧ GetHomeDomain (prot) ∈ GetDomainSet(prot)
> >
> > ∧ GetCurrentDomain (prot) ∈ GetDomainSet(prot)
>
> type: Protector → BOOL

12.9.2 Protector Operation: Access

```
Access (prot, objref, reqp) =
    ( let givenp =
      RetrieveProtection(GetCurrentDomain(prot),objref)
      in
       (IsAllowedUse (givenp, reqp)
            ⟶ RetrieveObject (bs, objref),
         true
            ⟶ Nil
       )
    )
```

type: Protector ObjectReference Protection ⟶ CRLObject

12.9.3 Protector Operation: AddProtectionDomain

```
    AddProtectionDomain (prot, pdom) =
        (PutDomainSet (GetDomainSet(prot) ∪ {pdom}))
```

type: Protector ProtectionDomain ⟶ Protector

12.9.4 Protector Operation: RemoveProtectionDomain

```
RemoveProtectionDomain(prot,pdom) =
    (PutDomainSet ( GetDomainSet (prot) − {pdom}))
```

type: Protector ProtectionDomain ⟶ Protector

12.9.5 Wellformedness Condition for ProtectionDomains

```
is-wf-ProtectionDomain (pdom) =
    ( ∀ or ∈ dom pdom )
        ((or ∈ dom bs) ∧
        (p = pdom (or)
        → is-wf-Protection (p, or)))
```

type: ProtectionDomain → BOOL

12.9.6 ProtectionDomain Operation: AddProtectedObject

```
AddProtectedObject (pdom, objref, p) =
( pdom + [ objref → p])
```

type: ProtectionDomain ObjectReference Protection → ProtectionDomain

12.9.7 ProtectionDomain Operation: RemoveProtectedObject

```
RemoveProtectedObject(pdom, objref) =
    (pdom − {objref})
```

type: ProtectionDomain ObjectReference → ProtectionDomain

12.9.8 ProtectionDomain Operation: Allow

```
Allow (pdom, objref, perm) =
( let t = GetTypeInfo (Retrieve Protection (pdom, objref)),
 sp = GetPermissions (RetrieveProtection(pdom, objref))
in
( is-wf-Permission (perm, t)
 →AddProtectedObject (pdom,
                    objref,
```

```
            PutPermissions (sp ∪ {perm}))))
```

type: ProtectionDomain ObjectReference Permission
                   →   ProtectionDomain

12.9.9 ProtectionDomain Operation: Disallow

Disallow (pdom, objref, perm) =
(let t = GetTypeInfo (Retrieve Protection (pdom, objref)),
    sp = GetPermissions (RetrieveProtection(pdom, objref))
in
  (is-wf-Permission (perm, t)
    ⟶AddProtectedObject (pdom,
                              objref,
                              PutPermissions (sp − {perm}))))

type: ProtectionDomain ObjectReference Permission
                   →   ProtectionDomain

12.9.10 ProtectionDomain Operation: RetrieveProtection

    RetrieveProtection(pdom,objref)=
        (pdom (objref))

type: ProtectionDomain ObjectReference   →   Protection

12.9.11 Wellformedness Condition for Protection

is-wf-Protection (p) =
    (∀ perm ∈ GetPermissions(p))
        (is-wf-Permission (perm, GetTypeInfo(p)))

type: Protection   →   BOOL

12.9.12 Protection Operation: IsAllowedUse

```
IsAllowedUse (givenp, reqp) =
( GetTypeInfo (givenp) ∈ CompatibleTypes (GetTypeInfo(reqp))
    ⟶
        ( let gr = union {rset| ∃ perm ∈ GetPermissions(givenp)
                              (rset = EvaluatePermission(perm))}
             rr = union {rset| ∃ perm ∈ GetPermissions (reqp)
                              (rset = EvaluatePermission (perm))}
    in
        rr ⊆ gr),
  true
    ⟶ false)
type: Protection  Protection    →     BOOL
```

12.9.13 Wellformedness Condition for Permission

This condition is not a standard wellformedness condition on Permissions, but a combined condition for a Permission object and a CRLType.

```
    is-wf-Permission (perm, t) =
    (EvaluatePermission(perm) ⊆
        GetPrincipalRights (t))
type:  Permission  CRLType    →     BOOL
```

12.9.14 Permission Operation: EvaluatePermission

```
    EvaluatePermission (perm) =
    (EvaluateControlExpression ( GetPermCondition(perm))
        ⟶ GetThenRights(perm),
    true
        ⟶ GetElseRights(perm))
type:  Permission    →      AccessRight -set
```

13. Shared Storage

13.1 Functional Requirements

- Support should be given to the reliable storage of persistent objects.

- Users should be provided with explicit possibilities for recovery where system recovery is not feasible.

- Concurrent use of operations on objects must be provided for in such a way that the semantics of the operations is not violated.

- The shared storage should contain all that information about objects which is not specific to a particular user's view of that object.

13.2 Overview

The Bonded Store models the universe of objects which are visible to the user. Objects are thereby treated independently from the way they are actually viewed by any single user, which is only possible on the basis of and relative to a Context as described in chapter 5. The Bonded Store also models the persistence of objects in the system, and those inherent properties of the objects which do not depend on the specific view of a single user.

In the design of a particular command and response language the designer may also care to incorporate the modelling of space consumption in refinements of the BondedStore, thus providing the basis for an accounting mechanism.

Therefore the Bonded Store contains not only objects which are created by a user (e.g. files), but also those objects of the model which are constituent parts of the command and response language system and the persistence of which is visible to the user: for example, Context, NameManager and Directory. Some other objects which are constituent parts of the system may not be contained in the Bonded Store, although they may also be replaced in a system, say in order to recover from a system crash. A pertinent example of this is the Bonded Store itself, which may be updated using back-up facilities after a system failure. The difference is that objects which are modelled as being held by the Bonded Store are those which may be subject to actions causing Create or Delete operations to be performed on them. Operations which are not contained in the Bonded Store are never subject to user actions which involve Create or Delete operations referring to them.

The decision as to which objects actually go into the Bonded Store, and which do not, relates to the actual command language design, because it depends on which objects the user can directly manipulate.

The Bonded Store is not necessarily a static repository of objects, since objects are subject to administration during their lifetime. Administration guarantees the existence of objects in case of spontaneous failures of system devices, by providing back-up for recovery, possibilities for overriding access rights, etc. It includes the organisation of migrating objects within the Bonded Store between different devices, and it includes accounting. Administration may be automated to a certain extent, i.e., be part of the system functions. Independently of the degree of automation, however, there remains the need of a specific administration interface for the objects of the user within the system. In particular, the human administrator may—in exceptional cases—delete an object despite the explicit wishes of the user. Though in principle administration can be modelled by sharing, the model allows administration to be subsumed to a certain extent as a property of the Bonded Store. In many systems administration is done by a "super user" with access to everything. This may be modelled with the mechanism for sharing and protection, but we have chosen not to elaborate this in detail.

Introducing a new object means more than simply storing the information. For each object, the Bonded Store contains all the information which is not solely dependent on the customised view of a specific user. In particular, all access routines which apply to a stored object are assumed to be part of the Bonded Store. But the access rights are kept separate in Protection objects because they may be different for different users of the same object (see Chapter 12). Therefore storing a new object rquires the two operations StoreObject and AddProtectedObject. Objects are normally accessed with the Protector operation Access, which first checks the legality of the desired access.

Introduction of an object requires that the object is associated with a CRL object type which can already be found in the Bonded Store. Thus the Bonded Store needs to deal with object types in addition to objects. In order to allow capabilities offered by general purpose systems of today, object types can also be introduced at run time of the system by a two-step procedure:

- definition of an object type (this models the introduction of the code for performing accesses to objects of a given type)

- instantiation of an object type (this models the instantiation of a type manager by providing system resources to the access routines of a given type).

Thereby the model allows for several simultaneous instantiations of the same kind of access routines in the system, distinguished by different names. Note, however, that those different names may not be visible to many users who view objects through individually tailored Contexts. For example, within different Contexts, alternative versions of a data management system may be accessed by issuing identical commands.

13.3 Object Type : Bonded Store

The BondedStore is modelled as a mapping from ObjectReferences to (CRL) objects. It is only accessible to users via Protector objects. There is only one instance of type BondedStore.

```
TYPE BondedStore = ObjectReference m → CRLObject
NEEDS TYPES  ObjectReference, CRLObject
DECLARE      or: ObjectReference
```

```
                  ob: CRLObject

                  bs: BondedStore

INTERFACES        RetrieveObject (bs, or) : CRLObject

                  StoreObject (bs, or, ob): BondedStore
```

END BondedStore

Semantics

RetrieveObject retrieves an object from the BondedStore, provided that the ObjectReference passed is in the domain of the storage mapping. Otherwise the Nil object is returned. This operation may be used only by Protector objects, and by NameManager objects in a strictly controlled way.

Store Object introduces a new pair ObjectReference - CRLObject into the BondedStore. If the ObjectReference was contained in the BondedStore previously, its old association will be overwritten with the new object.

13.4 Formal Interface Definitions

The following declarations are used:

> or: ObjectReference
> ob: CRLObject
> bs: BondedStore

13.4.1 BondedStore Operation: RetrieveObject

```
RetrieveObject (bs,or) =

     (or  ∈  dom bs  ⟶  bs (or),

          true       ⟶  Nil)


type:  BondedStore  ObjectReference   →    CRLObject
```

13.4.2 BondedStore Operation : StoreObject

```
StoreObject (bs, or, ob) =

    (bs + [ or  →  ob ])
```

```
type:  BondedStore  ObjectReference  CRLObject

                    →      BondedStore
```

References

[1] International Standards Organisation, Open Systems Interconnection - Basic Reference Model. IS 7498. 1983.

[2] J.P. Bourguignon, PCTE: A Basis for a Portable Common Tool Environment. In J. Roukens and J.F. Rennart (eds): ESPRIT '84: Status of Ongoing Work, Elsevier, 1985.

[3] O.-J. Dahl, K. Nygaard and B. Myhrhaug, The SIMULA 67 common base language, Norwegian Computing Center, Oslo, 1968.

[4] B. Liskov, R. Atkinson, T. Bloom, E. Moss, C. Schaffert, R. Scheifler and A. Snyder, CLU reference manual, Lecture notes in computer science, 114, Springer-Verlag, Berlin, 1981.

[5] W.A. Wulf, R.L. London and M. Shaw, An introduction to the construction and verification of Alphard programs. IEEE Transactions on Software Engineering, SE-2 (1976), 4.

[6] A.I. Wasserman, D.D. Sheretz, M.L. Kersten, R.P.van de Riet and M.D. Dippé, Revised report on the programming language PLAIN. ACM SIGPLAN Notices, 16 (1981), 5.

[7] D. Bjørner, O.N. Oest (eds), Towards a formal description of Ada, Lecture notes in computer science, 98, Springer-Verlag, Berlin, 1980.

[8] R.L. Bates et al., The Affirm Reference Library. Information Sciences Institute, University of Southern California, 1981.

[9] J.E. Archer, R. Conway, and F.B. Schneider, User Recovery and Reversal in Interactive Systems. ACM Transactions on Programming Languages and Systems, Jan 1984.

Appendix A : Notation

Object Type Specification

Every object type is described both in English language and in the more formal notation defined in this appendix. The formal notation is based on AFFIRM [6] and on the VDM metalanguage as defined in appendix B. The English part introduces the object type under consideration and explains its role in the reference model by relating it to other object types.

The formal specifications are to a large extent applicative, i.e., they are expressed as mathematical functions being applied to arguments and producing results, without reference to an underlying, permanent store defining an overall state of the system. This must be introduced when putting the model together, but most of the object types and operations may be semantically defined separately in an applicative way.

Syntax of Type Specification

The formal specification follows the syntax:

```
TYPE    < object type >  =  < type expr >
NEEDS TYPES   < type₁ > , ...
              < type₂ > , ...
                . . .
DECLARE   < name₁ >, ... :  < type₁ >
          < name₂ >, ... :  < type₂ >
            . . .
INTERFACES
    < fct.name₁ > ( < arg₁ >, ... ) :  < type expr₁ >
    < fct.name₂ > ( < arg₂ >, ... ) :  < type expr₂ >
    . . .
END  < object type >
```

For the syntax variables used above, the following rules hold:

< object type > is the identifier of the new type.

< type expr > is a domain expression as defined in appendix B. It is optional and may be omitted.

$< \text{type}_1 >$, $< \text{type}_2 >$, ... are identifiers of object types defined elsewhere, but used—directly or indirectly—in the specification of the interface operations.

$< \text{name}_1 >$, $< \text{name}_2 >$, ... and $< \text{arg}_1 >$, $< \text{arg}_2 >$, ... are identifiers, often chosen as 3-4 letter acronyms, denoting instances of objects occurring as arguments for the interface functions. All the argument names used in the INTERFACES must belong to the list $< \text{name}_1 >$, $< \text{name}_2 >$, ...

The type names $< \text{type}_1 >$, $< \text{type}_2 >$, ... used in the DECLARE section must occur in the NEEDS TYPES section or be the $< \text{object type} >$ name.

$< \text{fct.name}_1 >$, $< \text{fct.name}_2 >$, ... are identifiers denoting the basic operations on the object type.

$< \text{type expr}_1 >$, $< \text{type expr}_2 >$, ... denote the types of the results of the functions. They may be just type names $< \text{type}_1 >$, $< \text{type}_2 >$, ... , or they may be domains composed of these through domain expressions.

Errors and exceptions occurring in the function calls are treated as follows. With each type T, two functions are pre-defined:

ErrorT
is-ErrorT(obj) .

The result of the parameter-free function ErrorT is a special object of type T, which may be used to signal error or exception cases. If this result is used as an argument for another function of type U, the result of that function is the error object of that type, ErrorU. The second function is a Boolean function used to check whether the argument obj is the error object of that type.

Furthermore, there is one object Nil which belongs to all types. The semantics of Nil may be defined separately for each type, but an object may always be tested using the pre-defined Boolean function

is-Nil (obj)

where obj may be of any type.

Basic Operation Specification

For the basic operations in the INTERFACES part, a sub-section describes the semantics of the function in English language, and in several cases the semantics are also formally specified at the end of the chapter, using a subset of the VDM metalanguage.

The VDM specification is written as a function definition using the names of the arguments as given above. The form used most often is:

```
< fct.name > ( < list of arguments > ) =
( let
    < definition of local short-hand notations >
  in
  ( < case₁ >   ⟶   < result₁ > ,

    . . .

    < caseₙ >   ⟶   < resultₙ >
  )
)


    type:  < list of argument types >   ⟶   < result type >
```

In the list of arguments, the 'distinguished argument' (i.e., the object of the type being defined which is to be operated on) is placed first.

$< case_1 >$, ..., $< case_n >$ are Boolean expressions each defining one case (one branch) of the function evaluation, and the corresponding $< result_1 >$,... are functional expressions defining the result of the function in each case.

A number of the branches cover the exceptional cases. The result of an exceptional case is the error-flagged object of the type to which the function belongs. It is expressed as a call of the error function of that type. To test whether an object is 'in error', we shall use predicates of the form

    is-Error < object type > (< name >)

by analogy with the VDM predicates is-type.

For some object types the given domain expressions define domains which are too large. The domain of a type may be restricted through a well-formedness condition, and this is expressed as a predicate function

    is-wf- < object type > (obj) = < Boolean expression > .

Types consisting of a number of components are defined with the heading

    TYPE <object type > :: s- <id1 > : <component1 >
                             s- <id2 > : <component2 >

                    ...

and such a type has implicitly available operations for selecting each of the components:

    Get <id1 > (<object of this type >), ...

If the type is defined without selector-ids, we use the component names directly in the selector operations:

`Get` <component1 > (<object of this type >), ...

Likewise, Set <id1 > or Set <component1 > operations are implicitly available in these circumstances to be applied to (<object of this type >, <new value for component1 >), to return an object with this component altered to the new value and all other components unchanged.

Further details of the metalanguage notation are to be found in appendix B.

Appendix B : The VDM Metalanguage

This appendix is reprinted from [5] with the kind permission of Dines Bjørner. It describes the language used in the formal specification of operations.

1. DATA TYPES

The language constructs for expressing Domains of objects, for constructing and representing objects, and for operating upon objects are defined. Each subsection is accordingly presented in three parts. For operations we state their type, i.e. types of ordered input argument(s) and result value.

1.1. Elementary Data Types

1.1.1. The Boolean Data Type

Domain Expression : BOOL

BOOL denotes the Domain of truth values, i.e. the set : {true,false}.

Object Representation : true, false

Object Operations :

Symbol	Name	Type		
'	negation	BOOL		→ BOOL
∧	and	BOOL	BOOL	→ BOOL
∨	or	BOOL	BOOL	→ BOOL
⊃	implies	BOOL	BOOL	→ BOOL
≡	equivalent	BOOL	BOOL	→ BOOL

Operators ∨ and ∧ are not commutative. Thus :

$$a \lor b \triangleq \text{if } a \text{ then true else } b$$
$$a \land b \triangleq \text{if } a \text{ then } b \text{ else false}$$
$$a \supset b \triangleq \text{if } a \text{ then } b \text{ else true}$$
$$a \equiv b \triangleq \text{if } a \text{ then } b \text{ else (if } b \text{ then false else true)}$$

1.1.2. The Integer Data Type

Domain Expressions : INTG, N_0, N_1

INTG denotes the Domain of integer values, i.e. the infinite set : $\{...,-2,-1,0,1,2,...\}$. N_i denotes the Domain of positive integers larger than or equal to i.

Object Representation : $...,-2,-1,0,1,2,...$

Object Operations :

Symbol	Name	Type	
-	minus	INTG	→ INTG
abs	numerical	INTG	→ N_0
-	subtract	INTG INTG	→ INTG
+	add	INTG INTG	→ INTG
★	multiply	INTG INTG	→ INTG
/	integer division	INTG INTG	→ INTG
mod	modulus	N_0 N_1	→ N_0
=	equal	INTG INTG	→ BOOL
≠	different	INTG INTG	→ BOOL
<	less than	INTG INTG	→ BOOL
≤	< or equal	INTG INTG	→ BOOL
>	larger than	INTG INTG	→ BOOL
≥	> or equal	INTG INTG	→ BOOL

Integer division leads to the largest integer smaller than or equal to the real quotient. Modulus (of i,j) gives the largest natural number, r, less than j such that there exist a natural number multiplier m such that : $i = j \star m + r$.

1.1.3. The Quotation Data Type

Domain Expression :   QUOT

QUOT denotes the Domain of quotations; these are represented as any bold-face sequence of uppercase letters or digits.

Object Representation :   A, B, ... , Z, 0, 1, ... , AA, AB, ... , A9, AAA, ...

Object Operations :

Symbol	Name	Type	
=	equal	QUOT QUOT	→ BOOL
≠	different	QUOT QUOT	→ BOOL

(Two quotations are equal if they form exactly the same "sequence" (or "pattern") of characters.)

1.1.4. The Token Data Type

Domain Expression :   TOKEN

TOKEN denotes the Domain of tokens. This Domain can be considered as consisting of a potentially infinite set of otherwise distinct, elementary, i.e. further unanalysed objects for which no representations (designators) are required.

Object Representation :   -- not applicable (N/A)

Object Operations :

Symbol	Name	Type	
=	equal	TOKEN TOKEN	→ BOOL
≠	different	TOKEN TOKEN	→ BOOL

1.2. Composite Data Types

Composite objects are such which are composed from other objects. A composite data type (or Domain) has objects, all of which are composite. Whereas fixed names where prescribed for the elementary data type Domains, viz. : BOOL, INTG, TOKEN, and QUOT, the definer, if required, must use abstract syntax definition facilities to ascribe names to composite Domains. In all of the subsections below suitable decorated A's and B's denote arbitrary Domains. Suitable decorated a's and b's represent objects of corresponding Domains.

1.2.1. The Set Data Type

Domain Expression : A-set

-set is a suffix operator. As an operation, it applies to Domains, A, and yields the possibly infinite Domain of objects all of which are finite, possibly empty, subsets of A, i.e. unordered collections of distinct A objects.

Object Construction :

Explicit enumeration : $\{a_1, a_2, ..., a_s\}$
Implicit enumeration : $\{a \mid P(a)\}$, $\{a \; \varepsilon \; aset \mid P(a)\}$

Usually $s = 0$ or 1, i.e. $\{ \}$, which denotes the empty set of no (A) objects, respectively $\{a\}$, which denotes the singleton set of exactly one object. $\{a \; \varepsilon \; aset \mid P(a)\}$ is a short-hand for writing $\{a \mid a \; \varepsilon \; aset \wedge P(a)\}$. The ellipsis (...) is meta linguistic. The explicit enumeration lists all members of the set. The implicit enumeration constructs the (finite) set of all those objects which satisfy the predicate (see sect. 1.5.2) $P(a)$.

Object Operations :

Symbol	Name	Type	
ε	membership	A SET	$\rightarrow$ BOOL
$\cup$	union	SET SET	$\rightarrow$ SET
$\cap$	intersection	SET SET	$\rightarrow$ SET
$\setminus , -$	complement, difference	SET SET	$\rightarrow$ SET
$\subset$	proper inclusion, subset	SET SET	$\rightarrow$ BOOL
$\subseteq$	inclusion	SET SET	$\rightarrow$ BOOL
$=$	equal	SET SET	$\rightarrow$ BOOL
$\neq$	distinct	SET SET	$\rightarrow$ BOOL
card	cardinality	SET	$\rightarrow N_0$
union	distributed union	SET-set	$\rightarrow$ SET

If a is in the set $aset$ then $a \; \varepsilon \; aset$ holds. If the set $aset$ is empty then for no a does $a \; \varepsilon \; aset$ hold. If $aset$ is not empty then it is possible to extract an arbitrary member of $aset$: (let $a \; \varepsilon \; aset$ in ...).

$$as_1 \cup as_2 \triangleq \{a \mid a \; \varepsilon \; as_1 \vee a \; \varepsilon \; as_2\}$$
$$as_1 \cap as_2 \triangleq \{a \mid a \; \varepsilon \; as_1 \wedge a \; \varepsilon \; as_2\}$$
$$as_1 - as_2 \triangleq \{a \mid a \; \varepsilon \; as_1 \wedge a \; `\varepsilon \; as_2\}$$
$$as_1 \subset as_2 \triangleq (A \; a \; \varepsilon \; as_1)(a \; \varepsilon \; as_2) \wedge (E \; a \; \varepsilon \; as_2)(a \; `\varepsilon \; as_1)$$
$$as_1 \subseteq as_2 \triangleq (A \; a \; \varepsilon \; as_1)(a \; \varepsilon \; as_2)$$
$$as_1 = as_2 \triangleq (A \; a \; \varepsilon \; as_1)(a \; \varepsilon \; as_2) \wedge (A \; a \; \varepsilon \; as_2)(a \; \varepsilon \; as_1)$$
$$as_1 \neq as_2 \triangleq \; `(as_1 = as_2)$$
$$\text{card } as = (as = \{ \} \rightarrow 0, \; T \rightarrow (\text{let } a \; \varepsilon \; as \text{ in } 1 + \text{card } (as - \{a\})))$$
$$\text{union } sas = \{a \mid as \; \varepsilon \; sas \wedge a \; \varepsilon \; as\}$$
$$\{m : n\} = \{i \mid m \leq i \leq n\}$$

1.2.2. The Tuple Data Type

Domain Expressions : A^*, A^+

$*$ and $+$ denote (suffix) Domain operations which yield Domains of objects all of which are finite, possibly zero-, respectively non-zero-, length, ordered sequences (lists, tuples) of not necessarily distinct A objects.

Object Constructions :

Explicit enumeration : $\langle a_1, a_2, ..., a_t \rangle$
Implicit enumeration : $\langle F(i) \mid m \leq i \leq n \wedge P(i) \rangle$,
$\langle G(i) \mid i \; \varepsilon \; \{m : n\} \wedge P(i) \rangle$

Usually $t = 0$ or 1, which denotes the empty tuple of no (A) objects and zero length, respectively $\langle a \rangle$, which denotes the unit-length tuple of exactly the a object. The head, or first, $[1]$, element or object of the explicitly enumerated tuple is a_1; the second, $[2]$, is a_2, ... , with the t'th, $[t]$, being a_t. F and G are arbitrary functions defined over the domains for which P holds. The first object of the implicitly defined, F produced tuple is $F(j)$ where j is the smallest integer, in the range $\{m : n\}$, for which $P(j)$ holds. The next object is the $F(k)$ where k is the next-smallest, etc.. The last element is the $F(l)$ where l is the largest integer, in the range $\{m : n\}$, for which $P(l)$ holds. In the G

produced tuple no ordering of $G(i)$ elements is prescribed; thus any permutation of $<G(i) \mid m \leq i \leq n \wedge P(i)>$ is denoted.

Object Operations :

Symbol	Name	Type	
hd	head,first	A^+	$\rightarrow A$
tl	tail	A^+	$\rightarrow A^\star$
[.]	index	$A^+ \; N_1$	$\rightarrow A$
len	length	$A^\star$	$\rightarrow N_0$
elems	elements	$A^\star$	$\rightarrow A$-set
ind	indices	$A^\star$	$\rightarrow N_1$-set
^	concatenation	$A^\star \; A^\star$	$\rightarrow A^\star$
conc	distributed concatenation	$A^{\star\star}$	$\rightarrow A^\star$
=	equal	$A^\star \; A^\star$	$\rightarrow$ BOOL
≠	distinct	$A^\star \; A^\star$	$\rightarrow$ BOOL

The head of a non-empty tuple is its first element, the tail the tuple of remaining elements. Selecting the ith *tuple* element, for $1 \leq i \leq$ **len** *tuple*, yields that element :

$$tuple[i] \quad \triangleq \quad ((1 \leq i \leq \text{len } tuple) \rightarrow ((i = 1) \rightarrow \text{hd } tuple, \; T \rightarrow (\text{tl } tuple)[i-1]), \quad T \rightarrow \text{ undefined}),$$
$$\text{elems } tuple \triangleq \{tuple[i] \mid i \, \varepsilon \text{ ind } tuple\},$$
$$\text{ind } tuple \quad \triangleq \{i \mid 1 \leq i \leq \text{len } tuple\}.$$

Concatenation, $t_1 \; \hat{} \; t_2$, of two tuples, yields a tuple, t, whose ith element for $1 \leq i \leq$ **len** t_1 is the ith element of t_1, and for $i = j +$ **len** t_1, where $1 \leq j \leq$ **len** t_2, is the jth element of t_2.

$$\text{conc } tt \quad \triangleq \quad \text{if } tt = <> \quad \text{then} <> \quad \text{else hd } tt \; \hat{} \; \text{conc tl } tt.$$
$$t_1 = t_2 \quad \triangleq \quad (t_1 = <> \; \equiv \; t_2 = <>) \vee ((\text{len } t_1 = \text{len } t_2) \wedge (\text{hd } t_1 = \text{hd } t_2) \wedge (\text{tl } t_1 = \text{tl } t_2))$$

Where equality with empty tuples is assumed a primitive.

1.2.3. The Map Data Type

Domain Expression : $\quad A \; _m\!\!\rightarrow B$

$_m\!\!\rightarrow$ is an infix Domain operator. As an operation it yields the Domain of all finite, possibly empty domain, partial maps, i.e. finitely constructable functions, from objects in a subset of A into B. Partiality because not all of A need be the domains of denoted maps.

(Observe : 'Domain', spelled with capital 'D', is the name used for the concept of a possibly infinite set of objects defined by some Domain expression; whereas 'domain', spelled whith 'd', is the name used for the concept of the set of objects for which a function is defined, i.e. to which it applies & yields well-defined values.)

Object Construction :

Explicit enumeration : $\quad [a_1 \rightarrow b_1, a_2 \rightarrow b_2, ..., a_m \rightarrow b_m]$
Implicit enumeration : $\quad [F(o) \rightarrow G(o) \mid P(o)]$

Usually $m = 0$ or 1, i.e. [ ], which denotes the empty map, i.e. the totally undefined function, which functionally associates no A objects with any B object, respectively $[a \rightarrow b]$, which denotes the one domain element function which maps a into b. Assume F, G and P to denote A-, B- respectively BOOL object producing functions where F and G apply to all those O objects, o, for which at least $P(o)$ holds. Then the implicit map enumeration expression denotes a map which functionally associates, or "pairs", exactly those $F(o)$ objects with $G(o)$ objects for which $P(o)$ holds.

Object Operations :

Symbol	Name	Type
(.)	apply	$(A_m \to B)\ A \quad \overset{\sim}{\to} B$
U	merge	$(A_m \to B)\ (A_m \to B) \overset{\sim}{\to} (A_m \to B)$
+	override extend	$(A_m \to B)\ (A_m \to B) \overset{\sim}{\to} (A_m \to B)$
\	complement restrict (with)	$(A_m \to B)\ A\text{-set} \quad \to (A_m \to B)$
|	restrict (to)	$(A_m \to B)\ A\text{-set} \quad \to (A_m \to B)$
dom	domain	$(A_m \to B) \quad \to A\text{-set}$
rng	range	$(A_m \to B) \quad \to B\text{-set}$
=	equal	$(A_m \to B)\ (A_m \to B) \to \mathbf{BOOL}$
≠	distinct	$(A_m \to B)\ (A_m \to B) \to \mathbf{BOOL}$
merge	distributed merge	$(A_m \to B)\text{-set} \quad \to (A_m \to B)$

Let $m, m_1, m_2 \ \varepsilon\ (A_m \to B)$. If a is in the domain of m, i.e. if $a\ \varepsilon\ \text{dom}\ m$ holds, then $m(a)$ yields the b to which a is functionally associated, i.e. with which a is "paired".

If domains of m_1 and m_2 do not share A objects, then :

$$m_1 \cup m_2 \ \triangleq\ [a \to b \mid (a\ \varepsilon\ \text{dom}\ m_1 \wedge m_1(a) = b) \vee (a\ \varepsilon\ \text{dom}\ m_2 \wedge m_2(a) = b)]$$

If domains of m_1 and m_2 (potentially) overlap, then :

$$m_1 + m_2 \ \triangleq\ [a \to b \mid (a\ \varepsilon\ \text{dom}\ m_2 \wedge m_2(a) = b) \vee (a\ \varepsilon\ \text{dom}\ m_1 \setminus \text{dom}\ m_2 \wedge m_1(a) = b]$$
$$m \setminus aset \ \triangleq\ [a \to b \mid a\ \varepsilon\ \text{dom}\ m \setminus aset \wedge m(a) = b]$$
$$m \mid aset \ \triangleq\ [a \to b \mid a\ \varepsilon\ aset \cap \text{dom}\ m \wedge m(a) = b]$$
$$m_1 = m_2 \ \triangleq\ (\text{dom}\ m_1 = \text{dom}\ m_2) \wedge (\mathbf{A}\ a\ \varepsilon\ \text{dom}\ m_1)(m_1(a) = m_2(a))$$

Let $mab\ \varepsilon\ (A_m \to B)$ and $mbc\ \varepsilon\ (B_m \to C)$, then

$$mab \circ mbc \ \triangleq\ [a \to c \mid a\ \varepsilon\ \text{dom}\ mab \wedge mab(a)\ \varepsilon\ \text{dom}\ mbe \wedge mbc(mab(a)) = c]$$
$$\text{merge}\ sms \ \equiv\ ((sms = \{\ \}) \to \{\ \},\ \mathbf{T} \to (\text{let}\ m\ \varepsilon\ sms\ \text{in}\ m \cup \text{merge}(sms \setminus \{m\})))$$

provided $(\mathbf{A}\ m_1, m_2\ \varepsilon\ sms)((m_1 \neq m_2) \supset (\text{dom}\ m_1 \cap \text{dom}\ m_2 = \{\ \}))$, i.e. that any two distinct maps, of the set of maps merged, have disjoint domains.

Bijections : $\quad A \leftarrow_m \to B \quad\quad$ **(Domain Expression)**

A map is a bijection iff to each distinct range object there corresponds a distinct domain object. Let $m\ \varepsilon\ (A \leftarrow_m \to B)$, then for defined a, $(m(a) = b) \triangleq (m^{-1}(b) = a)$.

1.2.4. The Function Data Type

Domain Expressions : $\quad A \to B \quad\quad (A \overset{\sim}{\to} B)$

$A \to B\quad (A \overset{\sim}{\to} B)$ denote the Domain of all total (partial) functions from A ((i.e. subsets of A)) into B.

Object Construction :

1. $\quad \lambda a.C(a)$,
2. $\quad (\text{let}\ f(a) = C(a)\ \text{in} ...)$,
3. $\quad (\text{let}\ f = \lambda a.C(a)\ \text{in} ...)$,
4. $\quad (\text{def}\ f(a) : C(a); ...)$, etc.

Forms 1.-3. basically define the same function, namely : "that function of a which $C(a)$ is". Forms 2.-3. gives the name, f, to the defined function (with this name appearing free in the bodies ... of the block). Forms 2.-3. therefore permits the recursive definition of f; i.e. f to appear free in $C(a)$. Thus $(\text{let}\ f = \lambda a.C(a)\ \text{in} ...)$ is equal to $(\text{let}\ f = Yf.\lambda a.C(a)\ \text{in} ...)$ where the latter let is not recursive, but where Y is the least-fix-point finding function(al). Forms 1.-3. define applicative functions which rely on no state (see sect 1.3). Form 4. defines an imperative function since it is assumed that evaluation of $C(a)$ relies on the state. The f of forms 1.-3. returns a value, whereas the f of form 4. may return a value - potentially changing the state - , or may potentially change the state, not returning any value. In the former case f is a value-returning ("applicative") function, in the latter case f is a state-changing ("imperative") function. In the former case references, $f(arg)$, may occur anywhere an expression occurs; in the latter case anywhere a statement occurs. $C(a)$ is any clause, which for forms 1.-3. is an expression; for form 4. an expression, respectively a statement.

Form 1., when encountered during elaboration of a meta-program, and the right-hand-sides of the **let** and **def** specifications of forms 2.-4., are not elaborated. A function is (instead) defined which, if (and when) applied, to some argument, say *arg*, yields the same effect as would elaboration of C(*arg*) (i.e. where all free *a* in C(*a*) have been replaced by *arg*), in the defining environment, i.e. in the bindings present at the point of elaboration of the function definition.

Object Operation :

Symbol	Name	Type		
(.)	apply	$(A \stackrel{\sim}{\to} B) \, A$	$\stackrel{\sim}{\to} B$	

is the only operation defined on lambda (λ) defined functions. (Thus function objects cannot be tested for equality/distinction - and any such operation on other composite objects which involve functional ones is hence not defined.)

1.2.5. The Tree Data Type

Domain Expressions :

0.: $(B_1 \ B_2 \ ... \ B_n)$

Domain Definitions :

1.: $A_1 = (B_1 \ B_2 \ ... \ B_n)$ **(Abstract Syntax Rule)**
2.: $A_2 :: B_1 \ B_2 \ ... \ B_n$ **(Abstract Syntax Rule)**

Forms 0.-1. defines a Domain of anonymous, i.e. root-non-labelled, trees, whereas form 2. defines A_2-root-labelled, i.e. non-anonymous, trees. The defined trees all have exactly *n*, non-ordered, sub-components, of Domains $B_1, B_2, ... , B_n$.

Object Constructions :

0.-1.: $(b_1, b_2, ..., b_n)$ where $b_i \, \varepsilon \, B_i$
2.: $mk\text{-}A_2(b_1, b_2, ..., b_n)$ where $b_i \, \varepsilon \, B_i$

forms 0.-1. are interchangeably written as : $mk(b_1, b_2, ..., b_n)$.

Axiom :   **if :** $A_1 :: B_1 \ B_2 \ ... \ B_m$,
                 $A_2 :: C_1 \ C_2 \ ... \ C_n$,   and
                 $mk\text{-}A_1(b_1, b_2, ..., b_m) = mk\text{-}A_2(c_1, c_2, ..., c_n)$,
  then $A_1 \equiv A_2$,
                 $m = n$,
                 $B_i \equiv C_i$ for all $1 \leq i \leq m$,   and
                 $b_i = c_i$ for all $1 \leq i \leq m$.

This axiom secures disjointness of Domains of root-labelled trees labelled with distinct roots (A_1, respectively A_2).

Object Operations

Symbol	Name	Type		
$s\text{-}B_i$	select	A	$\to B_i$	
$=$	equal	$A \ A$	$\to$ **BOOL**	
$\not\equiv$	distinct	$A \ A$	$\to$ **BOOL**	

where A is either A_1 or A_2, or some such tree Domain.
   Let

         $t_1 = (b_1, b_2, ..., b_n)$
         $t_2 = mk\text{-}A_2(b_1, b_2, ..., b_n)$

and B_i be an identifier distinct from other identifiers B_j $(1 \leq j \neq i \leq n)$, then

$$s\text{-}B_i(t_1) = b_i = s\text{-}B_i(t_2)$$

Equality of trees holds only for trees of the same Domain, $(B_1 \ B_2 \ ... \ B_n)$, A_1 or A_2, i.e. let :

$$t' = mk\text{-}A_2(b_1',b_2',...,b_n')$$
$$t'' = mk\text{-}A_2(b_1'',b_2'',...,b_n'')$$

$t' = t''$ holds iff $b_i' = b_i''$ for all $1 \leq i \leq n$. Etcetera.

1.3. The Access Data Type and The State

Domain Expressions :   ref A

The Domain ref A is the Domain of all references, i.e. meta-locations, of variables declared of type A.

Object Constructions :   (dcl ra [:= expr] type A; ...)

ra is the name of an assignable, i.e. updateable, meta-variable. [its content may be initialized, to the value of expr.] Values of the location must always be of type A.

The State : Σ (Domain Name)

If the following declarations :

     dcl v_1 ... type A_1
     ...
     dcl v_2 ... type A_2
     ...
     ...
     ...
     dcl v_n ... type A_n

are in effect at a given point in the elaboration of a meta-program, then the state Domain is defined as :

$$(v_1 \ _m \rightarrow A_1) \ \cup \ (v_2 \ _m \rightarrow A_2) \ \cup \ ... \ \cup \ (v_n \ _m \rightarrow A_n)$$

(see sect. 2.1 for $\cup$). If e.g. v_i is recursively declared, i.e. there is a (potentially) indefinite number of v_i locations, all of type ref A_i, then the term :

$$(v_i \ _m \rightarrow A_i)$$

instead becomes :

$$(ref \ A_i \ _m \rightarrow A_i),$$

etcetera.

Object Operations :

Symbol	Name	Type	
c	contents	ref A	$\rightarrow (\Sigma \rightarrow (\Sigma A))$
:=	assignment	ref A A	$\rightarrow (\Sigma \rightarrow \Sigma)$

Let σ be the (hidden) state, then :

     c v $\equiv$ if $v \in$ dom σ then $(\sigma, \sigma(v))$ else undefined
     v := val $\equiv$ if $v \in$ dom σ then $\sigma + [v \rightarrow val]$ else undefined

1.4. The Process Instance Data Type

Domain Expression : Π , $\Pi(pid)$

Π denotes a possibly infinite Domain of process instance values, possibly identifying instances of the processor definition *pid*. See sect. 5.1.

Object Construction : not applicable, see however sect. 5.2.1

Object Operations :

Symbol	Name	Type	
=	equal	Π Π	→ **BOOL**
≠	distinct	Π Π	→ **BOOL**

For special uses of Π-objects see sects. 5.2.2-3.

1.5. Descriptor and Quantified Expressions

Although not defining new data types we here introduce some auxiliary expression forms.

1.5.1. Descriptor Expressions

Schema : $(\Delta obj \; \varepsilon \; Set)(P(obj))$

-- denotes the unique object in the *Set* for which the *P*redicate holds. If the predicate holds for several, or no, objects of *Set*, then the expression, as a whole is undefined.

1.5.2. Quantified Expressions

Schemas : 1.: $(A \; obj)(P(obj))$, $(A \; obj \; \varepsilon \; Set)(P(obj))$
2.: $(E \; obj)(P(obj))$, $(E \; obj \; \varepsilon \; Set)(P(obj))$
3.: $(E! \; obj)(P(obj))$, $(E! \; obj \; \varepsilon \; Set)(P(obj))$

The right-hand column specifies bound quantification. The schemas reads : 1.: for all objects, *obj*, [in the *Set*] it is the case that *P(obj)* holds; 2.: there exist at least one object [in the *Set*] for which the precicate holds; and 3.: there exists a unique object [in the *Set*] for which the predicate holds. The expressions all yield truth values, i.e. denote objects in **BOOL**. [The *Set* may be infinite.] For finite sets, *Set*, the schemas can be explained :

     Let $Set = \{o_1, o_2, ..., o_n\}$

     1.: $P(o_1) \wedge P(o_2) \wedge ... \wedge P(o_n)$
     2.: $P(o_1) \vee P(o_2) \vee ... \vee P(o_n)$

and :

     3.:   **if** $(E \; o_i \; \varepsilon \; Set)(P(o_i))$
                   then *(let $o_i \; \varepsilon \; Set$ be s.t. $P(o_i)$ in*
                         $(A \; o \; \varepsilon \; Set \setminus \{o_i\})(\neg P(o)))$
                   else false

In the clause :   **if** $(E \; obj)(P(obj))$
                   then   ...
                   else   ...

the free occurrences of *obj* in ... are considered bound by the quantified expression, so that e.g. 3. above reads:
                   if $(E \; o_i \; \varepsilon \; Set)(P(o_i))$
                   then $(A \; o \; \varepsilon \; Set \setminus \{o_i\})(\neg P(o))$
                   else false

Observe : $(A \; o)(P(o)) \equiv \neg(E \; o)(\neg P(o))$,
            $\neg(E \; o)(P(o)) \equiv (A \; o)(\neg P(o))$

2. ABSTRACT SYNTAX

2.1. Domain Expressions

Domain Operators

Symbol	Name	Sect-Reference
-set	power-Domain	1.2.1
*	tuple-Domain	1.2.2
+	tuple-Domain	1.2.2
$\vec{m}$	map-Domain	1.2.3
→	total-function-Domain	1.2.4
⇸	partial-function-Domain	1.2.4
(...)	anonymous-tree-Domain	1.2.5
ref	access-Domain	1.3
|	arbitrary, non-discriminated-union Domain	
[...]	Domain optionality	
U	non-discriminated-map-merge Domain	

Explanations : $A \mid B \equiv \{ab \mid ab \, \varepsilon \, A \lor ab \, \varepsilon \, B\}$. $[A] \equiv A \mid \{nil\}$, where nil is just an arbitrarily chosen symbol denoting itself! $(A_1 \vec{m} B_1) \cup (A_2 \vec{m} B_2)$ etcetera denotes the Domain of maps whose A_i domain objects (for i either 1 or 2) map into B_i objects (for pairwise i's either both $= 1$, or both $= 2$, etcetera). The → operators associate to the right, i.e. $(A_1 \rightarrow A_2 \rightarrow ... \rightarrow A_{n-1} \rightarrow A_n) \equiv (A_1 \rightarrow (A_2 \rightarrow (... \rightarrow (A_{n-1} \rightarrow A_n)...)))$ commute. Note that sometimes, as in above expressions, parentheses are used for breaking or indicating precedence (grouping), rather than for tree Domain construction; context shows which.

2.2. Rule Definitions

Schemas :

0.:	$A = B_1 \mid B_2 \mid ... \mid B_n$	
1.:	$B_1 :: C_{11} \, C_{12} ... C_{1 \, m1}$	See sect. 1.2.5
2.:	$B_2 :: C_{21} \, C_{22} ... C_{2 \, m2}$	- " -
...	...	
n.:	$B_n :: C_{n1} \, C_{n2} ... C_{n \, mn}$	- " -

Rule 0. defines A to denote the same Domain as its right-hand side expression, giving a "handy" way of naming it. Rules i (for $1 \leq i \leq n$) denotes distinct tree Domains (insofar as '$(B_j \equiv B_k)$ for $j \neq k$, etcetera).

Domain Function :   is-A, is-B_i (for $1 \leq i \leq n$)

Any rule defines a predicate function of the form **is-** composed with the left-hand side rule identifier :

is-$A(obj) \equiv (obj \, \varepsilon \, A)$
is-$B_i(obj) \equiv (obj \, \varepsilon \, B_i)$

3. FUNCTION DEFINITIONS

Schema :
$$fid(p_1, p_2, ..., p_m)(s_1)(s_2) ... (s_n) =$$
$$Clause(...)$$
$$\text{type: } P_1 \, P_2 \, ... \, P_M \rightarrow (S_1 \rightarrow (S_2 \rightarrow ... \rightarrow (S_N \rightarrow D)...))$$

Commas in the formal parameter lie, as in ALGOL 60, be replaced by back-to-back parentheses : ")(". The type clause specifies the function type : parameters p_j are of type P_j, s_j of type S_j, and applying the function to arguments of corresponding types $(P_1 - P_m, S_1 - S_n)$ yields an object of type D. Elaboration of the function, named *fid*, proceeds by elaborating its body, *Clause(...)*, in which all free occurrences of formal parameters have been replaced by corresponding actual arguments. If that elaboration accesses, but does not change, the state, and returns a value of type E, then the type clause part "$\rightarrow D$" reads : "$\rightarrow (\Sigma \, E)$", for short "$=> E$". If the elaboration, in addition, changes the state "$\rightarrow D$" reads : "$\rightarrow (\Sigma \rightarrow (\Sigma \, E))$", for short "$=> E$". Thus we shall consider "$\rightarrow (\Sigma \rightarrow E)$" only as an abbreviation for "$\rightarrow (\Sigma \rightarrow (\Sigma \, E))$", permitted whereever there is no (chance of) state change. If elaboration alone potentially changes the state the part : "$\rightarrow D$" reach "$\rightarrow (\Sigma \rightarrow \Sigma)$", for short "$=>$". The *Clause* can be any expression or statement, inclusive blocks.

The function definition header *fid(mk-D(a,...,w))(...) = Clause(...)* is an abbreviation for : *fid(p)(...) = (let mk-D(a,...,w) = p in Clause(...))*.

3.1. Blocks

Schemas : 0.: (let *id* = *expr* in *Clause*)
1.: (def *id* : *expr*; *Clause*)
2.: (dcl v [:= *expr*] type *A*; *Clause*)

Form 0. applicatively defines all free occurrences of *id* in *Clause* to denote what expr denotes; as such form 0. is a short-hand for *Clause'* where all free occurrences of *id* in *Clause* have been syntactically replaced by '*expr*'. Form 1. imperatively defines all free occurences of *id* in *Clause* to denote the value of '*expr*', elaborated before elaboration of *Clause*; hence semicolon in form 1. means: "first evaluate *expr*, then bind *id* to that value, then elaborate *Clause* in the context of that binding". Form 1. is used wherever evaluation of *expr* requires access to a potentially changing state. Form 2. imperatively declares a variable, named v, possibly initializes it to the value of *expr*, fixes the type of variable values to *A*, and then elaborates *Clause*.

3.1.1. Let Clause Variants

Variants to the let clause of form 0. above and its use are often found useful:

Schemas : 1.: (let *id* ε *Set* [be s.t. *P(id)*] in ...),
2.: (let mk-*B*($b_1, b_2, ..., b_n$) = *tree* in ...),
3.: (let $id_1 = e_1$,
    $id_2 = e_2$,
    ...
    $id_n = e_n$ in ...),   and
4.: (let *f(a)* = *e* in ...)
5.: (let $id_1 = e_1$ in
   let $id_2 = e_2$ in
   ...
   let $id_n = e_n$ in ...)

Form 1. reads: let *id* be (the name of) an object in *Set* [for which the Predicate holds]. Form 2. assumes $B :: B_1 \, B_2 \, ... \, B_n$ and corresponds to form 3. where $id_i \equiv b_i$ and $e_i \equiv s\text{-}B_i(tree)$. Form 3. simultaneously defines n quantities. Forms 0., 1., 3. and 4. permit recursive definitions of *id*, *id*, id_i's, respectively *f*. If there are no mutually recursive definitions of any id_i in 3., then form 3. corresponds to form 5. which is an abbreviation of:

5.: (let $id_1 = e_1$ in
   (let $id_2 = e2$ in
   ...
   (let $id_n = e_n$ in ...)...))

Form 4. was explained in sect. 1.2.4.

3.2. Statement Composition

3.2.1. Sequential Statement Composition

Schema : $(s_1; s_2; ...; s_n)$

s_i, for all i, are statements. These are to be interpreted in the order listed. (See however sect. 4.)

3.2.2. [Quasi-] Parallel Statement Composition

Schema : $//(s_1, s_2, ..., s_n)$

s_i, for all i, are statements. These are to be interpreted in parallel. [In order not to confuse this "parallelism" with the notion of meta-processes, see sect. 5, you may choose to constrain the above to "quasi-parallel"; that is: operations of all s_i are serially performed, in any order, while preserving operator precedences.]

3.3. The Assignment Statement

Schema : $v := expr$

The value of *expr* replaces the current value of v, see sect. 1.3.

3.4. Function References

Schema : $fid(arg_1, arg_2, ..., arg_n)(d_1)(d_2)...(d_n)$

If the type of the *fid* function definition, see begin sect. 3., has "$\rightarrow$ D" containing no mention of the state Domain Σ, then *fid* is an applicative function, and the above form is an expression. If "$\rightarrow$ D" is of the form: "$=> E$" then *fid* is an "applicative" function accessing (and possibly changing) the state, and the form is an "imperative" expression. If "$\rightarrow$ D" is of the form "$=>$", i.e. "$\rightarrow$ $(\Sigma \rightarrow \Sigma)$", then fid is an imperative function, and the form is a statement. For further details see beginning of section 3.

3.5. The error Clause

Schema: error

Indicates a semantically erroneous construct. As used in this definition it indicates an error which must be detected.

3.6. The undefined Clause

Schema: undefined

Indicates a construct to which no semantics is (can be) given. As used in this definition it indicates an error situation which should not necessarily be detected.

3.7. Structured Clauses

3.7.1. Conditional Clauses

3.7.1.1. If-then-else

Schema :   **if** e **then** c_c [**else** c_a]

e is any expression evaluating to **true** or **false**. If to true then the *consequent clause*, c_c, is elaborated; otherwise the *alternative clause*, c_a. If c_c is an expression, then the else part is mandatory and c_a and the entire construct are expressions. If c_c is a statement and if c_a is present, it too is a statement; the entire construct is a statement.

3.7.1.2. McCarthy Conditional

Schema : $(e_1 \rightarrow c_1, e_2 \rightarrow c_2, ..., e_n \rightarrow c_n),$ $n \geq 2$

is semantically explained by translation into: (**if** e_1 **then** c_1 **else** (**if** e_2 **then** c_2 **else** (**if** ... **then** (... **else** (**if** e_n **then** c_n **else** *not-defined*)...)...))). If the e_n is T then the innermost phrase above reads: **else** c_n.

3.7.1.3. Cases

Schema :   **cases** e_0 : $(e_1 \rightarrow c_1, e_2 \rightarrow c_2, ..., e_n \rightarrow c_n)$

Is explained by translation into: (**let** $v = e_0$ **in** $((e_1 = v) \rightarrow c_1, (e_2 = v) \rightarrow c_2, ..., (e_n = v) \rightarrow c_n)$, respectively (**det** v : e_0; $((e_1 = v) \rightarrow$ ... etc.), depending on whether evaluation of e_0 does not or do require access to the state.
     A case construct of the form: **cases** e_0 : (mk-$D(a,...,w) \rightarrow c_1$, etc.) is explained as follows: (**let** $v = e_0$ **in** (is-$D(v) \rightarrow$ (**let** mk-$D(a,...,w) = v_0$ **in** c_1, etc.)).

3.7.2. Iterative Statements

3.7.2.1. Indexed Iteration

Schema :   **for** $i = m$ **to** n **do** $S(i)$

$S(i)$ is any statement; m and n are integer, usually natural number, valued, expressions (where m usually is 1 and n of the form **len** *tuple*). The expression evaluation usually is 'static', i.e. does not require access to the state. Let j and k be the values of m, respectively n, then the semantic is explained by translation into: $(S(j); S(j + 1); ...; S(k - 1); S(k))$, where for $j > k$ the whole thing collapses to I.

3.7.2.2. Un-ordered Iteration

Schema :   **for all** $id \, \varepsilon \, Set$ **do** $S(id)$

$S(id)$ is any statement, id an identifier free in the context, and Set a set-valued, usually 'static', expression. Let the value of Set be $\{o_1, o_2, ..., o_n\}$, in any order, then the semantics can be explained by translation into: $(S(o_1); S(o_2); ...; S(o_n))$. [The definer should be ready to assert that any ordering of Set leaves the effect invariant.]

3.7.2.3. Conditional Iteration

Schema :   **while** e **do** S

e is a boolean valued expression usually dependent upon the state for its evaluation; S is any statement. The semantics can be explained by repeated "translation": (**if** e **then** (S; **while** e **do** S) **else** I).

Index of Terms